MACMILLAN · FIELD · GUIDES

·ASTRONOMY·

A STEP-BY-STEP GUIDE
TO THE NIGHT SKY

Hartford – 7-3-89

3 hrs. – 27 min
To – John

The author

Storm Dunlop, a Fellow of The Royal Astronomical Society and a Council Member of The British Astronomical Society, is the author of numerous books on astronomy and meteorology. He lives in England.

Acknowledgements

Photographs

The photograph on page 34 is reproduced by kind permission of George Philip & Son Limited.
Ron Arbour, Bishopstoke; N Bone; Bretmain Ltd; British Museum, London; D Buczynski;
California Institute of Technology and Carnegie Institution of Washington; Charles Capen-Hansen
Planetarium; Salt Lake City, Utah; Celestron International, Torrance, California; B Cobley;
N Dogliani; A P Dowdell, Winchester; Storm Dunlop, East Wittering; D Gavine, Edinburgh;
J D Greenwood; Hamlyn Group – Steve Larsen; Alan Heath, Long Eaton; M J Hendrie, Colchester;
Kitt Peak National Observatory, Tucson; Lick Observatory, University of California, Santa Cruz;
Robert McNaught, Prestwick; B Manning; Michael Maunder; D Miles; D Miles/McInerney;
P Montgomery; Museum of the History of Science, Oxford; NASA, Washington, DC; A Page,
Brisbane; P Parviainen; H B Ridley, Yeovil; Royal Observatory, Edinburgh; John Sanford, Orange,
California; M Swan; Space Frontiers, Havant; United States Naval Observatory, Washington, DC.

Drawings

Richard Baum; J D Greenwood; Richard McKim;

Designed and illustrated by Templar Publishing

Macmillan Publishing Company
866 Third Avenue, New York, N.Y. 10022
Collier Macmillan Canada, Inc.

Library of Congress Cataloging in Publication Data

Dunlop, Storm.
  Astronomy.

  (Macmtillan field guides)
  Bibliography: p.
  Includes index.
  1. Astronomy – Observers' manuals. I. Title.
  II. Series
  QB63.D92   1985   523   84-17579

ISBN 0-02-079650-1

MACMILLAN · FIELD · GUIDES

·ASTRONOMY·

A STEP~BY~STEP GUIDE TO THE NIGHT SKY

STORM DUNLOP

Collier Books

Macmillan Publishing Company

New York

Contents

Section One: **Beginning Astronomy**

Section Two: **Exploring the Sky**

Over page: *The Veil Nebula in the constellation of Cygnus, part of the vast remnant of an ancient, stellar explosion.*

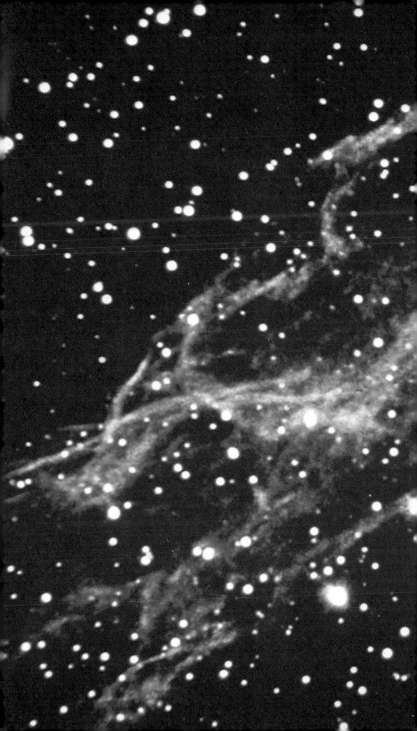

Beginning Astronomy

How to begin

Astronomy is a fascinating hobby that can be followed by anyone. You do not need to be, as some people seem to imagine, 'mathematically-minded', in order to start, or even to become a very experienced observer. Yet astronomy is one of the few hobbies where not only can you gain great enjoyment, but if you feel you want to, you can very easily make observations of great scientific value.

What may perhaps be even more surprising is that you do not need complicated equipment – or indeed any equipment at all. So if you are a beginner, do not feel that you must rush out and buy the most expensive telescope that you can afford. This could be a big mistake, as it might prove to be completely unsuitable for the objects which you later find are most interesting. If you must buy anything, a pair of binoculars are certainly far more useful at first, but even these are not essential, and some of the things that

can be observed with the naked eye are described on page 26. Similar lists of objects and observations that you can make with binoculars and photographs are given on pages 57 and 99, while details of how to choose (and test) binoculars and telescopes are given on pages 57 and 61, respectively.

How to use this book

There is such a range of objects that there is always something to see, from meteors and aurorae in the Earth's atmosphere, planets and stars, out to the distant galaxies far off in space. There is a lot of pleasure to be gained from 'rambling' around the sky, looking at whatever objects happen to be available at the time, or which take your fancy. Everyone must start in this manner, by learning to find their way, and recognizing the different constellations, so that

The constellations of Crux and Carina, showing the Coalsack Nebula, the most distinct of the dark clouds that lie along the Milky Way, and the η Carina nebula.

is how this book begins, as well as giving general information on how to set about observing.

Most astronomers find, after a while, that they become particularly interested in a few classes of objects, on which they tend to concentrate their attention. As these may require different types of equipment, or different methods of observation, they are individually described in the various sections of the second half of this book.

All the different objects and the methods by which they are best observed, as well as what can be seen or studied with particular equipment may be a little confusing, especially to beginners. A number of flow-charts and tables have therefore been given, which it is hoped will help you to find the relevant sections where the different subjects are discussed, and to move on to the next stage in discovering the fascination of astronomy.

Beginners

Naked-eye observing	**page 26**
Finding one's way around the sky	**page 34**
Binoculars	**page 56**
Making detailed observations	**page 92**
Keeping records	**page 92**
How to make drawings	**page 93**
How to take astronomical photographs	**page 96**

Starting to observe

There are a few things to remember when you start to observe, but first make sure that you are warm and dry – no-one can observe properly if they are uncomfortable. Even in summer it can get quite cold at night, so wear plenty of clothing. Dampness (especially underfoot) makes the problem worse, so a dry site is better than standing on wet grass. Stone and concrete can become very cold, and hard to the feet during a long observing session, so wooden duckboards which provide a bit of insulation are ideal. Try to pick a spot which also offers some protection from the wind, not only because it will be warmer, but also because the wind can shake binoculars or telescope, making viewing more difficult. Even a simple windbreak can help a lot. Dampness as it affects equipment is discussed later (page 18). Observers in warmer locations have other problems and may find that mosquito repellent is an essential part of their equipment.

The eyepieces of many telescopes can assume awkward positions and heights at times, so you may need some form of steps. These must be sturdy and stable, but reasonably easy to move. A stout wooden box may be a

This photograph of Saturn, one of the finest taken from Earth, is similar to the view through a good amateur telescope.

satisfactory alternative. Diagonals (page 74) can help to make the eyepiece more accessible. Looking high overhead is easier if you use a reclining, garden chair rather than craning your neck – and it is also far more comfortable.

It also helps to have everything to hand. Some telescope tripods incorporate space for small items, but a garden table is better for all the bits and pieces that you may want.

Eyesight

The pupil of the eye responds almost instantaneously to major changes in the light, but true **dark adaptation** takes place when a pigment (known as 'visual purple') builds up inside the retina. This takes about 30 minutes or more, and the eyes slowly become more sensitive. It helps if the eyes are protected from bright lights before you go out to observe – some observers put on sunglasses. Bright light quickly destroys dark-adaptation at any time – even viewing the Moon through a telescope will do this – but a very dim red light has least effect, so make sure that you have one for examining charts and writing notes. Cover a suitable lamp or pen-light with red paper or plastic, and either change the bulb to a dimmer one, or make sure that the covering lets through only a weak light.

The advantage of binocular observing is that you use both eyes at once, in the normal relaxed manner. With a telescope, try to conquer the natural tendency to close the 'unwanted' eye, which only leads to strain on both. With practice one eye can be 'ignored', but if this proves too difficult, or if there is a lot of stray light causing interference, wear an eyepatch that allows you to keep both eyes open.

The most troublesome eyesight defect is astigmatism (page 65), which can cause stellar images to appear elongated or misshapen. Long- or short-sight does not pose many problems, as most binoculars and telescopes have sufficient range of focusing adjustment for this to be accommodated. If spectacles have to be worn all the time, take particular care in selecting equipment (pages 57 and 71).

At first most beginners wonder if there is something wrong with their eyesight when they cannot see faint planetary detail, or pick out the dimmer stars. But it is surprising how quickly one's perception improves with practice, so the more frequently you can observe the better. Experienced observers frequently use **averted vision** – looking slightly to one side of the faint object they want to see, so that the image falls on a more sensitive part of the retina. This does work, although exact positions may become a little more difficult to judge. Although telescopes and binoculars should be as rigid as possible, very slight motion of the eyepiece can sometimes bring faint stars into view, as the eye picks up the movement.

The star clouds of the Milky Way in Sagittarius, a wonderful sight in low-power binoculars.

Where to observe

A dark observing site is most important. Interference from light prevents the proper dark adaptation that is so important for seeing faint objects. However, naked-eye and binocular observers have an advantage in that they can move around more freely than anyone with a telescope. Observing from within the shadow of a wall or building can make a great deal of difference. In towns and cities, not only is the light pollution very bad, but often only part of the sky can be seen, restricting the objects which are visible. Taking a portable telescope out into the country may be one answer, but with perseverance, much observing can be carried out even under poor conditions, and it may be an advantage when learning the constellations if only the brighter stars can be seen through city lights.

When to observe

Not all astronomy is done at night. Apart from the study of the Sun (page 139), which needs special techniques for the sake of safety, it is sometimes of advantage to study Venus in the daylight, when the contrast between its brilliance and the sky is reduced, and faint details are easier to see. In some observational fields it is important to try to make observations as soon as possible after the Sun has set, or immediately before it rises – searching for comets (page 169) and novae (page 177) are just two examples.

Calculating the time of sunrise or sunset, depending as it does upon one's position on Earth, is too complex to describe here. Due to the effects of **refraction**, when the Sun appears to be on the horizon, it is actually below it

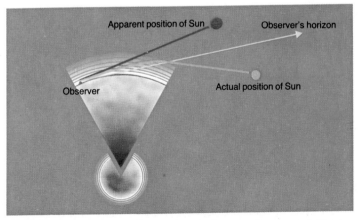

Curved light-paths produced by refraction in the atmosphere cause all astronomical objects to appear higher in the sky. The Sun and Moon also seem flattened when near the horizon.

Sunset. More than an hour must elapse before the sky becomes completely dark and the faintest astronomical objects can be seen.

by about 35 minutes of arc (approximately the same as its diameter). Newspapers and diaries often give the time of sunset and 'lighting–up' time, at the end of **civil twilight**, when the Sun is 6° below the horizon, as well as the corresponding times in the morning. Although a useful guide, these are local standard or summer times and are correct for only a few observers. More

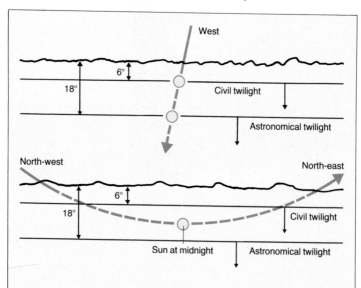

At low latitudes (top: south of the Equator) the Sun sets at a steep angle and astronomical twilight occurs every night, unlike the conditions in summer farther towards the poles (bottom: northern hemisphere).

important to astronomers is the length of **astronomical twilight** which occurs while the Sun is less than 18° below the horizon. It is only when astronomical twilight has ended (or has yet to begin) that it is fully dark. Astronomical twilight lasts at least 70 minutes after sunset and before sunrise. At moderately high latitudes – in fact beyond 48·5° N and S – astronomical twilight persists all night during some part of the summer months. An astronomical yearbook will give details of how long twilight lasts at your latitude on any particular date. However, observers at high latitudes have some compensations as it is in summer that noctilucent clouds (page 112) are likely to be seen. They are also most favoured with aurorae (page 110). In addition, it is sometimes more difficult to see objects near the Sun if observers are situated close to the equator, as the objects set more rapidly.

Moonlight also causes considerable interference with many types of observation, mainly because the scattered light increases the brightness of the background sky, reducing the contrast between it and the faint light of galaxies and similar objects. It may mean, for example, that meteor showers may be well-nigh unobservable in some years if they occur at the time of Full Moon. For those not interested in the Moon, a total lunar eclipse (page 133) can offer the chance of snatching a few valuable observations which would otherwise be unobtainable!

Light from the Moon – here shown aged 24 days – can cause serious interference to the observation of faint objects, which are best observed around New Moon.

Observations of superior planets – those outside the orbit of the Earth – and of the minor planets (sometimes called the asteroids), are usually best undertaken when they are close to opposition (page 54), crossing the meridian (page 22) at around midnight. Opposition is also the time when they are closest to the Earth, and offer the largest disk sizes (page 145). Mercury and Venus, the inferior planets, are best placed at elongation (page 54), when they are half-illuminated. Naturally, observations are also undertaken at other times, and with some objects, such as comets (page 168), there can be no choice of best observing period. The most favourable conditions for stars (page 170), clusters (page 179), nebulae (page 182), and galaxies (page 186) are when they cross the meridian at midnight and are highest in the sky.

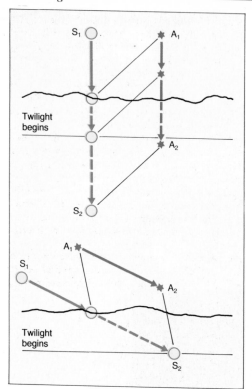

At the equator (top) an object A, close to the Sun, is well below the horizon by the time astronomical twilight begins. At high northern latitudes (bottom) the object is still easily observable the same length of time after sunset.

Atmosphere and seeing

Not all nights are equally suitable for observing, and the overall conditions (or **seeing**) are rated on a scale devised by Antoniadi, a famous planetary observer. Much depends upon meteorological conditions, including those

Antoniadi Scale of Seeing

I	Perfect seeing, without a quiver
II	Slight undulations, with moments of calm conditions lasting several seconds
III	Moderate seeing, with greater air tremors
IV	Poor seeing, with constant troublesome motion
V	Very bad seeing, scarcely allowing the making of even a rough sketch

high overhead, but very local effects caused by the observatory, telescope, and observer are also involved. When there is strong turbulence, variations in the density of the air layers refract light and produce **scintillation**. This gives rise to random movements of the images and changes in their brightness. Planetary disks appear blurred, and if stars are close to the horizon, where refraction disperses the light, they may show marked changes in colour – one of the causes of many so-called 'UFO' reports. In a telescope the effects are more pronounced and images wander around, and go in and out of focus. Under such conditions it may be necessary to persevere, and await the moments when the seeing steadies, although this may not happen very often during the course of a night. Naturally, photography and serious observing may well be impossible under extreme conditions, which frequently occur on cold nights, even when the air near the ground appears to be calm.

The tube currents (page 63) found in some reflectors, and air turbulence within an observatory (page 75) have the same general effect. If equipment (particularly telescopes) is not kept in an unheated observatory or store it should be allowed to reach the same temperature as the outside air before observing begins, to help to prevent these problems.

There is always **absorption** in the atmosphere – it is sometimes called atmospheric extinction – decreasing the brightness of astronomical objects. This absorption is at a maximum close to the horizon, and decreases towards

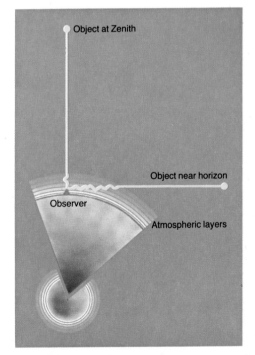

Object at Zenith

Object near horizon

Observer

Atmospheric layers

Objects close to the horizon show greater scintillation than those near the zenith as the light has a longer path through the dense, fluctuating, lower layers of the atmosphere.

the zenith (page 20). General haziness due to dust or pollution (especially downwind of a large, or industrial, city) degrades the seeing even more. Absorption can often be a problem with naked-eye observations, particularly estimating the magnitudes of variable stars (page 174) and meteors (page 117) at low altitudes, so take extra care under such conditions. Generally observations of even the brighter stars and planets are impossible within 10° of the horizon.

Large bodies of water do have a stabilizing effect upon local temperatures and conditions, and can noticeably improve seeing conditions. A slightly damp and even slightly hazy atmosphere can give rise to superb, steady conditions, and these also occur after rain, when the air has been washed clean of impurities. Although a damp haze may sometimes appear unfavourable, users of binoculars and telescopes often find that they can 'see through it' and experience good viewing conditions. Although patchy cloud-cover may be infuriating, it can frequently bring good conditions between the clouds. In general, cumulus clouds which build up during the day, have a tendency to die away and disperse after dark, but layer clouds, such as those associated with depressions, usually persist into the night. Some of the best seeing conditions come with the passage of cold fronts, even though the air behind may still contain a fair amount of cloud.

Dampness can also be a problem when it produces condensation, or **dewing**, on telescopes, binoculars, and other items, if they become colder than the surrounding air, or are taken into a warm atmosphere. Dewcaps (page 66) should always be used, and objectives and mirrors must be covered before being taken indoors. If a glass surface does become dewed, it should not be wiped, with the risk of damage to the optical coating, but the dampness may be dispersed by fanning with a piece of paper.

Under good conditions (below) faint objects can be seen and resolution is high, but with poor seeing (opposite above) many details and faint stars are lost.

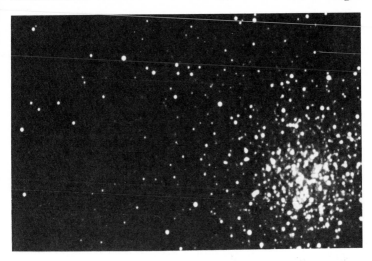

Essential equipment

The only items which are essential are a red light, and a notebook and pen or pencil. (A pencil is always worth having anyway, as some ball-point pens refuse to write if it is cold.) Try to keep a note of what you observe – even if it is only to record that some object was, or was not, visible. It is a good habit, too, to enter the date and time of every observation, so a watch or clock is also needed, preferably one set to Universal Time (page 90) to prevent confusion. Try making little sketches of planets, lunar features, galaxies or anything else that takes your fancy. They don't have to be great works of art, but just good enough to give an impression of what you can see. Gradually, as you build up your knowledge of the sky, your notes and drawings will become better, more comprehensive, and probably more specialized. It may seem like a chore, but actually they will quickly add to your enjoyment of the hobby. (Keeping records is more fully described on page 92.)

What equipment do you possess?

None	Naked-eye observing	**page 26**
	Choosing binoculars	**page 57**
Binoculars	Observing with binoculars	**page 59**
	Choosing a telescope	**page 61**
Telescope	Using telescopes	**page 66**
Camera	Photography	**page 96**

The celestial sphere

The stars and all other celestial bodies, such as the Sun and Moon, appear to be located on the inside of a vast sphere, centred on the observer, and rotating towards the west. Although we know that this view – which of course was held by the ancients – is not true, it is still a useful way of thinking about the sky. Just as latitude and longitude are used to locate positions on the surface of the Earth, a system of celestial co-ordinates (page 77) are used on the celestial sphere. The north and south celestial poles are extensions of the Earth's rotational axis, and the celestial equator is in line with the Earth's equator.

The observer's position on Earth

Exactly which part of the celestial sphere is ever visible depends upon the observer's position on the Earth. At the North Pole only the northern portion of the sky – and thus half of the stars – can be seen, and of course a similar situation applies at the South Pole. In both cases every star in that half of the sky is visible whenever the Sun is below the horizon, and the heavens rotate about the corresponding celestial pole, which is found at the **zenith**, directly overhead. The bright star Polaris (α Ursae Minoris) is very close to the true position of the northern celestial pole, but unfortunately in the south the pole is not marked by any conspicuous star.

At other latitudes, stars from both northern and southern celestial hemispheres can be seen. At 45° north, for example, Polaris appears half-way

The altitude of the poles is always equal to the observer's latitude. At 45° N (below),
Capella is just circumpolar, but at 35° S (opposite below), Canopus sets for part of the night
and Crux brushes the horizon.

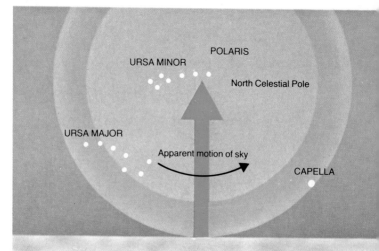

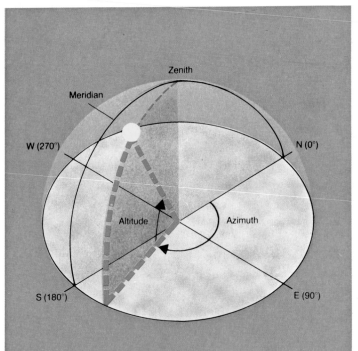

Above: *Altitude is always measured upwards from the plane of the horizon, and azimuth around from the north point towards the east.*

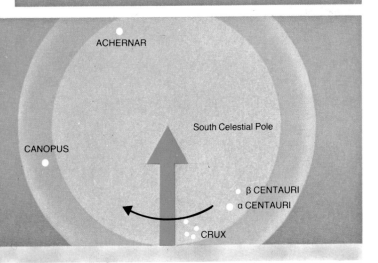

down towards the northern horizon, and many of the southern stars are visible. Now however, only the stars within 45° of the celestial pole remain above the horizon all the time, or are **circumpolar**, being seen on any clear night. The remaining stars rise and set, and those that are visible throughout the course of a night change slowly with the seasons. In theory anyone at the equator could see both poles and all the stars in the sky (although only half at once), but in practice the effects of refraction and absorption (page 17) complicate the issue.

For any observer the most important imaginary line in the sky is the **meridian**, which is a great circle running right round the sky through the north and south poles and the observer's zenith. It also passes through the **nadir**, the point directly below the observer's feet, and may be regarded as the celestial equivalent of the observer's meridian of longitude on the surface of the Earth. As objects cross this north-south line they are said to **transit** the meridian. (Transit telescopes, fixed to observe just this line in the sky, were once important equipment at every observatory.) An object **culminates**, reaching its highest altitude in the sky, as it transits the meridian. Circumpolar stars, of course, cross the meridian both above and below the pole, and these events are known as upper and lower culmination, respectively.

Because the sky appears as a sphere, centred on the observer, all distances between objects can be expressed as angles, 360° forming a complete circle. It is frequently useful to be able to make these measurements, even if only approximately. When the location of any object has to be specified exactly with respect to the observer's horizon, the co-ordinates **altitude** and **azimuth** are employed. An astrocompass can be used, but a device capable of measuring these angles to a sufficient degree of accuracy for most purposes is very simple to make and well worth constructing.

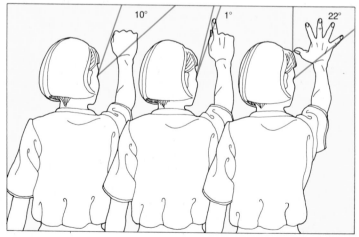

Angles may be estimated approximately by using a hand at arm's length, the results being correct for nearly everyone.

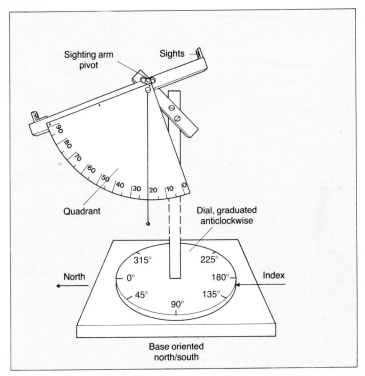

A simple device for measuring altitude and azimuth. A plumb–line gives the altitude, azimuth being read from the graduated disk that moves with the upright.

Changes throughout the year

The Earth's true rotation period, measured with respect to the stars (the **sidereal day**), is about four minutes shorter than the Sun's average, apparent rotation period (the **mean solar day**), due to the Earth's motion around the Sun. As a result, when measured by ordinary civil time, individual stars rise (and set) about four minutes earlier each day, slowly shifting westwards across the night sky. At times they may come too close to the Sun to be visible (page

Conversion of celestial co-ordinates to angles

RA	units of arc	RA	units of arc
24ʰ	360°	1ᵐ	15′
1ʰ	15°	4ˢ	1′
4ᵐ	1°	1ˢ	15″

54), thus giving rise to unavoidable seasonal gaps in observation.

We know that stars actually move in space, and change their positions relative to one another. However, their distances from us are so great that any changes due to this **proper motion** take centuries to become apparent to the

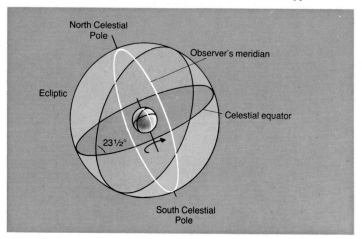

Above: *On the celestial sphere the poles and the equator are directly related to those of the Earth. As the Earth rotates the whole sky passes across any observer's meridian during the course of a day.*

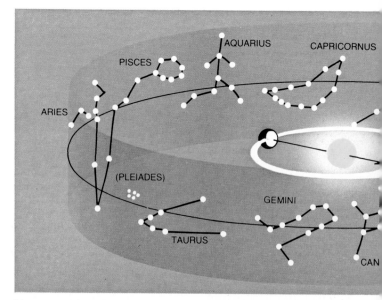

naked eye. For most purposes we can imagine that the Sun, Moon, planets, and other bodies move against this 'fixed' background. The Sun appears to trace out a path known as the **ecliptic**, completing the circuit of 360° in one year. Because the Earth's axis is tilted by just under 23·5°, the ecliptic makes the same angle with the equators of the Earth and of the celestial sphere. During the course of the year this naturally gives rise to the changing elevation of the Sun, and to the seasons.

The Moon and major planets follow paths which usually lie within about 8° of the ecliptic. In ancient times there were twelve constellations in this band (about 16° wide), and these formed the Zodiac of the ancient astrologers, and were regarded as having special significance. With the passing of the centuries, and the effects of precession (page 78), the position of the ecliptic has altered with respect to the background stars. The Sun and planets may appear in constellations such as Ophiuchus (the Serpent Bearer) – an ancient constellation – which are not included in the Zodiac. It is small wonder then, that astronomers regard astrology and 'star-signs' as sheer superstition. Only one of the symbols for the zodiacal constellations is in common use by astronomers, that for Aries (♈), which is used to indicate one of the two important points upon the celestial sphere where the ecliptic crosses the celestial equator (page 78).

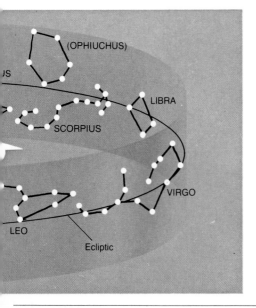

Left: *The band of the Zodiacal constellations in which the Moon and planets may be found is centred on the ecliptic, the Sun's apparent path.*

Naked-eye observing

There are many things that you can do with just the naked eye. Most important is learning the constellations and how to find your way around the sky, as described shortly (page 34). This is essential for any astronomer, and provides excellent practice for later binocular and telescopic observing. The same applies to many individual objects. The Moon, for example, shows about the same amount of detail to the naked eye as most of the planets do through small telescopes, so making drawings of the Moon (page 93) can be very useful experience.

Many stars are distinctly coloured (page 170) and several of the open and globular clusters (page 179) are visible, as are a few of the external galaxies (page 186). The star clouds of our own Galaxy appear as the Milky Way, which runs right around the celestial sphere. Its beauty can only be truly appreciated with the naked eye, observing in dark skies. You can then also trace its dark clouds without great difficulty. Any instruments give too high a magnification for its full extent to be seen, so that only wide-field cameras do it any justice. Frequently too, the tails of comets (page 168) can only be distinguished without any optical aid at all (or else only with very specialized equipment), as they are so faint and of such low contrast.

It is a test for the eyesight to see if some stars appear double (page 177), and there are some variable stars (page 173) – apart from occasional novae (page 176) – which either rise above the naked-eye limit, or can be seen all the time. Spotting the thinnest crescent of the New Moon is also a challenge, and it is

Naked-eye objects

Const.	Desig.	Name and remarks
And	M31	Great Andromeda Galaxy
Cnc	M44	Praesepe – open cluster
CVn	M3	Globular cluster
Cen	ω	Fine globular cluster
Cru	κ	Coal-sack – dark nebula
Dor/Men	LMC	Large Magellanic Cloud – nearest galaxy
Her	M13	Globular cluster
Lyr	ε	Double to very good eyesight
Ori	M42	Orion Nebula
Per	h & X	The Double Cluster – twin open clusters
Per	M34	Open cluster
Tau	θ	Easy double star
Tau	M45	Pleiades – finest open cluster
Tuc	SMC	Small Magellanic Cloud
Tuc	47	Globular cluster – NGC 104
UMa	ζ	Mizar – wide double with Alcor

supposed to be possible to see the satellites of Jupiter (page 163) with good eyesight, under very favourable conditions.

The major planets (page 54) may usually be readily recognized, and both the large, but distant Uranus (page 166) and the minor planet Vesta (page 158) may be at about the limit of naked-eye visibility under good seeing conditions. The movements of planets and comets may be followed over a period of time and plotted against the stars.

Perhaps the most important observations that can be made, however, are those of meteors (page 113) and aurorae (page 110). Efficient observation of the former, in particular, requires a good knowledge of the constellations.

The progress of a lunar eclipse is just one of the observations that can be carried out by the naked eye.

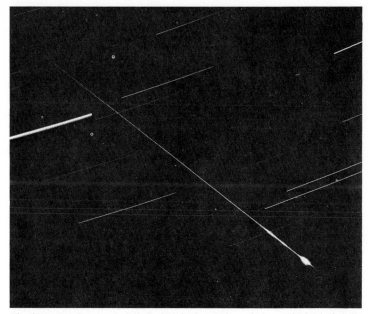

The observation of meteors is an ideal subject for those without telescopes. This bright fireball was a member of the annual Perseid meteor shower.

Learning the constellations

If you are interested in astronomy it is essential to be able to find your way around the sky, and it is best to begin by learning some of the most important groups of stars, or **constellations**. There are 88 of these and their names form a rather odd mixture as some date back to antiquity and commemorate mythological beings and creatures, and others are of far more recent origin, frequently describing scientific instruments. The patterns of stars hardly ever bear even the slightest resemblance to the objects after which they have been named, and in general the individual stars are at greatly different distances and are quite unrelated to one another, so that they merely appear to be close together.

Both the constellation boundaries and the official names were only settled by international agreement in 1930, and some of the older names are still occasionally encountered. The Quadrantid meteor stream (page 114) is called after the constellation (no longer existing) of Quadrans Muralis, for example. In addition to its proper, Latin name (often derived from earlier Greek words), nearly every constellation has a common name, frequently just a translation from the Latin. Most astronomers use the Latin names, and these are given in the table, together with some of the more common, colloquial names that are occasionally found, especially in older books. If you are learning the constellations for the first time, try to use the Latin names, even though they may seem a little more difficult to remember or to pronounce, as they are internationally-known and are found in all the most useful charts and catalogues. Don't be put off by the thought that 88 different constellations and names may be too many to learn, because as we have seen (page 20), the part of the sky that is visible varies with the observer's position on Earth, and also depends upon the season (page 23) and the time of night (page 91). Many constellations may therefore be permanently, seasonally, or temporarily invisible. In any case it is quite easy to learn one new constellation every night.

Once the major constellations are known and recognized, you will find that the fainter ones are soon distinguished. Occasionally one or more planets may appear in a constellation, and make it difficult to recognize – at least at first glance. This can only happen to the constellations along the ecliptic (page 25), and the planets are usually easy to recognize from their appearance, and because they show less tendency to scintillation (page 17) than neighbouring stars. Their motions over a period of time also serve to identify them, and these are discussed later (page 54).

Old constellation maps, such as this one by Hevelius from the mid-seventeenth century, only included the brightest stars and irregular constellation boundaries.

Table of Constellations

Name	Genitive	Abbreviation	Common Name
Andromeda	Andromedae	And	Andromeda
Antlia	Antliae	Ant	The Air Pump
Apus	Apodis	Aps	The Bird of Paradise
Aquarius	Aquarii	Aqr	The Water Carrier
Aquila	Aquilae	Aql	The Eagle
Ara	Arae	Ara	The Altar
Aries	Arietis	Ari	The Ram
Auriga	Aurigae	Aur	The Charioteer
Boötes	Boötis	Boo	The Herdsman
Caelum	Caeli	Cae	The Graving Tool
Camelopardalis	Camelopardalis	Cam	The Giraffe
Cancer	Cancri	Cnc	The Crab
Canes Venatici	Canum Venaticorum	CVn	The Hunting Dogs
Canis Major	Canis Majoris	CMa	The Greater Dog
Canis Minor	Canis Minoris	CMi	The Lesser Dog
Capricornus	Capricorni	Cap	The Goat
Carina	Carinae	Car	The Keel
Cassiopeia	Cassiopeiae	Cas	Cassiopeia
Centaurus	Centauri	Cen	The Centaur
Cepheus	Cephei	Cep	Cepheus
Cetus	Ceti	Cet	The Whale
Chamaeleon	Chamaeleonis	Cha	The Chameleon
Circinus	Circini	Cir	The Pair of Compasses
Columba	Columbae	Col	The Dove
Coma Berenices	Coma Berenicis	Com	Berenice's Hair
Corona Australis	Coronae Australis	CrA	The Southern Crown
Corona Borealis	Coronae Borealis	CrB	The Northern Crown
Corvus	Corvi	Crv	The Crow
Crater	Crateris	Crt	The Cup
Crux	Crucis	Cru	The Cross
Cygnus	Cygni	Cyg	The Swan
Delphinus	Delphini	Del	The Dolphin
Dorado	Doradus	Dor	The Dorado
Draco	Draconis	Dra	The Dragon
Equuleus	Equulei	Equ	The Foal
Eridanus	Eridani	Eri	The River Eridanus
Fornax	Fornacis	For	The Furnace
Gemini	Geminorum	Gem	The Twins
Grus	Gruis	Gru	The Crane
Hercules	Herculis	Her	Hercules
Horologium	Horologii	Hor	The Pendulum Clock
Hydra	Hydrae	Hya	The Water Snake
Hydrus	Hydri	Hyi	The Lesser Water Snake
Indus	Indi	Ind	The Indian

Name	Genitive	Abbreviation	Common Name
Lacerta	Lacertae	Lac	The Lizard
Leo	Leonis	Leo	The Lion
Leo Minor	Leonis Minoris	LMi	The Lesser Lion
Lepus	Leporis	Lep	The Hare
Libra	Librae	Lib	The Scales
Lupus	Lupi	Lup	The Wolf
Lynx	Lyncis	Lyn	The Lynx
Lyra	Lyrae	Lyr	The Lyre
Mensa	Mensae	Men	The Table Mountain
Microscopium	Microscopii	Mic	The Microscope
Monoceros	Monocerotis	Mon	The Unicorn
Musca	Muscae	Mus	The Fly
Norma	Normae	Nor	The Level
Octans	Octantis	Oct	The Octant
Ophiuchus	Ophiuchi	Oph	The Serpent Holder
Orion	Orionis	Ori	Orion
Pavo	Pavonis	Pav	The Peacock
Pegasus	Pegasi	Peg	Pegasus
Perseus	Persei	Per	Perseus
Phoenix	Phoenicis	Phe	The Phoenix
Pictor	Pictoris	Pic	The Painter's Easel
Pisces	Piscium	Psc	The Fishes
Piscis Austrinus	Piscis Austrini	PsA	The Southern Fish
Puppis	Puppis	Pup	The Stern
Pyxis	Pyxidis	Pyx	The Mariner's Compass
Reticulum	Reticuli	Ret	The Net
Sagitta	Sagittae	Sge	The Arrow
Sagittarius	Sagittarii	Sgr	The Archer
Scorpius	Scorpii	Sco	The Scorpion
Sculptor	Sculptoris	Scl	The Sculptor
Scutum	Scuti	Sct	The Shield
Serpens	Serpentis	Ser	The Serpent
Sextans	Sextantis	Sex	The Sextant
Taurus	Tauri	Tau	The Bull
Telescopium	Telescopii	Tel	The Telescope
Triangulum	Trianguli	Tri	The Triangle
Triangulum Australe	Trianguli Australis	TrA	The Southern Triangle
Tucana	Tucanae	Tuc	The Toucan
Ursa Major	Ursae Majoris	UMa	The Great Bear
Ursa Minor	Ursae Minoris	UMi	The Lesser Bear
Vela	Velorum	Vel	The Sail
Virgo	Virginis	Vir	The Virgin
Volans	Volantis	Vol	The Flying Fish
Vulpecula	Vulpeculae	Vul	The Fox

STARS Most of the brightest stars (page 172) have individual names, many of which were given by Arabic astronomers in the Middle Ages. These tend to be a bit confusing (as similar names apply to different stars), as well as being awkward to remember and, in some cases, well-nigh impossible to pronounce. However, astronomers very rarely use these

A fourteenth-century, Persian celestial globe. It is made of brass with inlaid silver 'stars'.

old names nowadays, except in a very few, particularly important cases, preferring to use the Greek-letter designations given by the German astronomer Bayer at the beginning of the 17th century. Bayer took each constellation in turn, generally calling the brightest star Alpha (α), the next brightest Beta (β), the third Gamma (γ), and so on down towards fainter stars, and through the alphabet (page 40). This system has been retained as it is so convenient, even though it only applies to the brightest stars, and despite the fact that in many cases we now know that the stars should have been arranged in a slightly different order of brightness. Various other methods of identifying the fainter stars have been used, and some of these schemes are discussed later (page 77).

The twin clusters in Perseus were once thought to be single stars and were therefore given the names h and χ Persei, which are still used.

The Bayer letter for an individual star is always followed by the Latin name of the constellation concerned, written in the genitive. These genitives are also given in the table (page 30), as are the standard three-letter abbreviations. The latter are nearly always used in lists of objects, and are probably easier to remember than the genitives. You will find that these, and the various other names soon become very familiar. As an example of how the system works we may take Mintaka, a star nearly on the celestial equator, in the constellation of Orion. The name Mintaka is derived from the Arabic *Al Mintaka*, 'the Belt', it being the northernmost of the three forming Orion's 'belt'. Bayer decided that it was fourth in importance in the constellation so called it 'δ (Delta) Orionis', usually written by astronomers as 'δ Ori'.

The brightness of stars (or of any astronomical objects, such as planets) is measured in **magnitudes**. For the moment it is sufficient to note that the scale works backwards, so that the brightest stars have the smallest magnitudes. Once again this is due to the ancient astronomers, who regarded the brightest stars as being the most important, and therefore of the 'first magnitude', the next brightest of the 'second magnitude', and so on. Under good conditions the faintest stars which can be seen with the naked eye are about magnitude six. The magnitude scale now has a sound scientific basis (page 172), but a few very bright objects had to be given negative values, such as $-1\cdot4$ for Sirius, the brightest star. Venus, the brightest planet, may reach magnitude -4, while the brightness of the Full Moon is about magnitude -13.

A planisphere shows which part of the sky is above the horizon at any date and time, so it is easy to determine which objects will be visible during the night.

Finding one's way around the sky

The star charts in this book are given in two forms. The first set are designed to help you to find your way around the sky and to recognize the major constellations. They emphasize the patterns formed by the brighter stars, not just those of the conventional constellations. Two charts cover the northern and southern circumpolar regions and six the equatorial band. For ease of initial identification the order of the equatorial charts is slightly different from that usually given. A later section explains the system of co-ordinates that enables the position of any object to be stated precisely (page 77), and the second set of charts (pages 80-87), carries these co-ordinates. Both sets show all the constellations and stars to fifth magnitude. The individual charts in the two sets cover the same regions of the sky, so they may be directly compared with one another.

Most observation is carried out in the evening, so the charts indicate when the particular regions are on the meridian at 21:00 hours (9 p.m.) local standard time (page 90). For every two hours earlier (or later) that you observe, a date one month earlier (or later) will be approximately correct. A device known as a **planisphere**, showing a flat projection of the sky, and with a rotating mask that can be set to any date or time, is very useful for showing which constellations are visible at any instant. You should be able to obtain one that is correct for your latitude.

The motions of the planets (page 54) are not easy to give for an extended period of time. Some approximate details are given in the tables for each planet, but full information has to be taken from a handbook or almanac for the year concerned.

The constellation with which observers begin depends mainly upon where they live on Earth. If you live in the Northern Hemisphere, Ursa Major (the Great Bear) is undoubtedly best, while in the Southern, Crux (the Southern Cross) is very distinctive. Orion and most other equatorial constellations are known to observers all over the world. Several prominent groups of stars (or asterisms) which are not true constellations in themselves, are also very useful for guidance in some regions of the sky.

The descriptions use the Latin names of the constellations, the standard, three-letter abbreviations and occasionally the genitives. These are all given in a table (page 30). Similarly, the actual Greek-letter names of stars are shown on the charts and given in the text. Occasional mention is made of the angular distance between particular stars. Methods by which such angles may be either estimated approximately, or else measured with reasonable accuracy using simple devices, are described on page 22. It is important to remember that in these descriptions – and in dealing with any star chart – compass directions do not refer to points around the observer's normal horizon but to the celestial sphere. 'North' is always towards the North Celestial Pole, and 'south' away from it, even with circumpolar constellations that may appear 'upside down'. Similarly, looking south along the meridian between the two celestial poles, 'west' is to the right.

Finding one's way around the sky

The northern polar constellations

The seven main stars of Ursa Major (UMa) form the group usually known as the 'Plough', and in North America as the 'Big Dipper', as well as by many other names. It is familiar to people who know nothing else about astronomy. The distinctive shape is easy to recognize, and it is usually visible at some time during the night, although on winter evenings it may be low on the northern horizon – and thus obscured – depending upon the latitude of where you live.

The two 'Pointers', β UMa (Merak) and α UMa (Dubhe), indicate the position of Polaris, the Pole Star, in Ursa Minor (UMi). The distance between the two Pointers is about 5°, and that from α UMa to Polaris is roughly 28°. Polaris (α UMi) is the one star that appears motionless in the sky. All the other stars seem to circle anti-clockwise around it very slowly throughout the night (page 20). In fact it lies about 1° from the north celestial pole, and does trace its own small circle. Its visual brightness is about magnitude 2, similar to the other bright star in Ursa Minor, β UMi (Kochab).

If you imagine a line from ζ UMa (Mizar: a naked-eye, binocular and telescopic binary) through Polaris, this passes very close to the true celestial pole. When extended by about the same distance, this line points to δ Cas, in the 'W'-shaped constellation of Cassiopeia (Cas), lying in the Milky Way. Starting at Polaris and moving anti-clockwise, mentally draw a line at right-angles to the one running from Mizar to Cassiopeia. This runs between the bright stars Deneb (α Cygni), and Vega (α Lyrae) slightly farther from the pole. Returning to the Plough or Big Dipper, the top of the 'bowl' (δ and α UMa) points unmistakably towards the constellation of Auriga (Aur) and the bright star Capella (α Aur).

The faint constellation of Draco (Dra) straggles around the pole and Ursa Minor, its quadrilateral 'head' lying north-east of Vega, and its 'tail' between Polaris and Ursa Major. The unremarkable, roughly pentagonal, constellation of Cepheus (Cep) lies partly in the Milky Way between Cygnus and Cassiopeia, extending up towards the pole. The brightest star α Cep is indicated by the line from α to β Cas.

On the other side of Cassiopeia, between it and Auriga and still in the Milky Way, lies the rather more obvious constellation of Perseus (page 48). The insignificant groupings of Camelopardalis (Cam) and Lynx (Lyn), and some of the fainter stars of Ursa Major lie in the large area between the seven main stars of that constellation and Auriga.

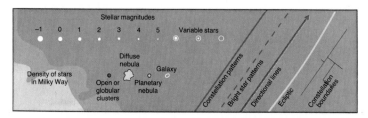

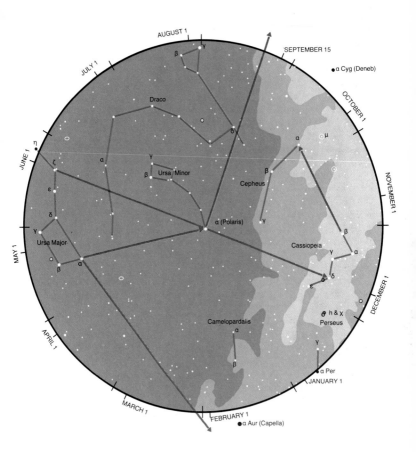

● α Lyr (Vega)

AUGUST 1

SEPTEMBER 15

● α Cyg (Deneb)

JULY 1

OCTOBER 1

β   γ

Draco

δ

α   μ

η

JUNE 1

NOVEMBER 1

ζ

α   γ

β   Cepheus

ε

β   Ursa Minor

δ

α (Polaris)

γ   β

Ursa Major

Cassiopeia

MAY 1

γ   α

β   α

δ

Perseus ε

β   α

h & χ

Perseus

DECEMBER 1

APRIL 1

Camelopardalis

α

γ

α Per

JANUARY 1

β

MARCH 1

FEBRUARY 1

● α Aur (Capella)

Equatorial constellations
January, February, March

Orion (Ori) is the key constellation in this region, and with its distinctive shape straddling the celestial equator, is a guide for northern and southern observers alike. The red supergiant star Betelgeuse (α Ori) and the brighter, brilliant white Rigel (β Ori) are distinctive, as is the line of three second-magnitude stars forming the 'belt' of this mythical hunter. The northernmost (δ Ori) lies nearly on the celestial equator. South of the belt are the stars of the 'sword' with the famous Orion Nebula (M42) in the centre. The nebula is faintly visible as a hazy patch even to the naked eye. Follow the line of the belt stars southwards and they point approximately towards Sirius (α Canis Majoris), the brightest star in the sky, with a magnitude of −1·4 (page 172). To the northwest the line of the belt passes just south of orange Aldebaran (α Tauri) with the nearby 'V' of the Hyades. Still farther to the west, the same line leads to the other very distinctive cluster in Taurus, the Pleiades (page 180).

The constellation of Taurus (Tau), although supposed to represent a bull, largely consist of a 'head' (Aldebaran and the Hyades) and 'horns', the tips of which are marked by single moderately bright stars, north of Orion, between that constellation and Auriga. Apart from these, there are a few fourth-magnitude stars which lie to the south and west of Aldebaran.

Auriga appears to form an irregular pentagon, although the southernmost star is actually β Tau. Bright Capella (α Aur) has the distinctive triangle of the 'Kids' to the east. The Milky Way runs through the constellation, but is less distinct here than in Cygnus, or in the dense star clouds of the southern hemisphere.

Northeast of Orion lies the Zodiacal constellation of Gemini (Gem) with the distinct bright pair of stars Castor (α Gem) and Pollux (β Gem). Pollux, the southernmost, is the brighter of the pair. Lines of stars running back towards Orion form the 'bodies' of the 'twins'. A line from δ UMa through β UMa, the southernmost of the two Pointers, also indicates Castor and Pollux.

South of Castor and Pollux, and forming more or less an equilateral triangle with Betelgeuse and Sirius, is the isolated bright star Procyon (α CMi) in the small constellation of Canis Minor (CMi), containing only one other bright star (β CMi), to the northwest. Canis Major (CMa), on the other hand, has several bright stars apart from Sirius, including one (ε CMa) of first magnitude.

The 'spine' of Canis Major points along the Milky Way, and a right-angle turn at ζ Puppis leads, past the 'two triangles' of Puppis, on to brilliant Canopus (α Carinae) the second-brightest star in the sky, magnitude −0·7. Between this and Orion lie the constellations of Columba and Lepus.

The constellation representing a river, Eridanus (Eri), begins at a third-magnitude star (β Eri) just north and west of Rigel, and winds its long way south in a chain of faint stars, none of which is brighter than magnitude 3, finally ending off to the west at first-magnitude Achernar (α Eri) even farther south than Canopus.

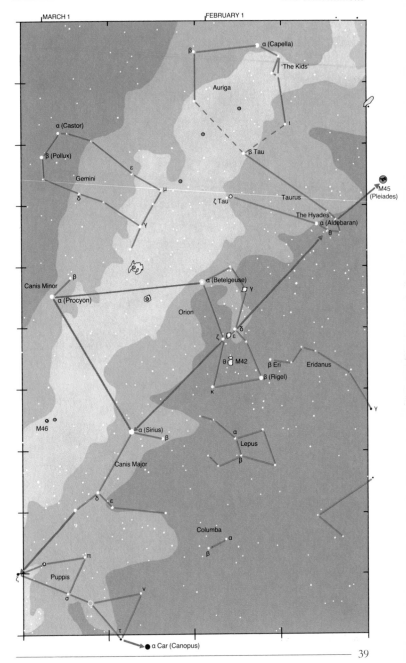

Equatorial constellations
March, April, May

South of Ursa Major (follow the line of the Pointers away from Polaris) and well to the east of the constellations of Gemini and Canis Minor, is the distinct constellation of Leo. Regulus (α Leo), the brightest, is a first-magnitude star almost on the ecliptic and may sometimes be occulated by the Moon (page 135). It forms part of the well-known asterism of the 'Sickle', a reversed 'question-mark' of stars, curving north and to the west. The main body of the constellation extends to the east towards second-magnitude Denebola (β Leo).

A line running through Regulus and Denebola is one way of finding bright, orange Arcturus (α Boötis) far off in the east. To the north of Leo, between it and Ursa Major lie Lynx (Lyn), with one third-magnitude star, and the very faint, uninteresting Leo Minor (LMi). Another small, faint constellation, Cancer (Cnc), lies between Gemini and Leo, and is only really notable for the Praesepe open cluster (M44).

South of Cancer and east of Procyon (α CMi) is the small asterism forming the 'head' of Hydra. Although actually the largest constellation in terms of area, Hydra (Hya) has only one bright star, Alphard (α Hya), southeast of Regulus. (Castor and Pollux actually point to both the 'head' and Alphard.) From there the constellation trails first south, then eastwards, roughly parallel to the equator, in a string of faint stars which ends even farther east than Arcturus.

Three faint constellations lie north of Hydra. The most insignificant is Sextans – its brightest star is magnitude 4·5 – lying south of Regulus, and northeast of Alphard. The next, Crater, lies to the southeast, west of the rather more conspicuous quadrilateral formed by the stars of Corvus.

There are brighter stars in the south. There the 'False Cross' (page 50) contains stars from Vela (Vel) and Carina (Car). The arm formed by ι Car and δ Vel points north to γ Vel, a striking double, and onwards approximately to ζ Puppis. Other first-magnitude stars in Vela are κ, also part of the 'False Cross' and orange λ Vel to the north.

Greek alphabet

letter	name	letter	name	letter	name
α	alpha	ι	iota	ρ	rho
β	beta	κ	kappa	σ	sigma
γ	gamma	λ	lamda	τ	tau
δ	delta	μ	mu	υ	upsilon
ε	epsilon	ν	nu	φ	phi
ζ	zeta	ξ	xi	χ	chi
η	eta	ο	omicron	ψ	psi
θ	theta	π	pi	ω	omega

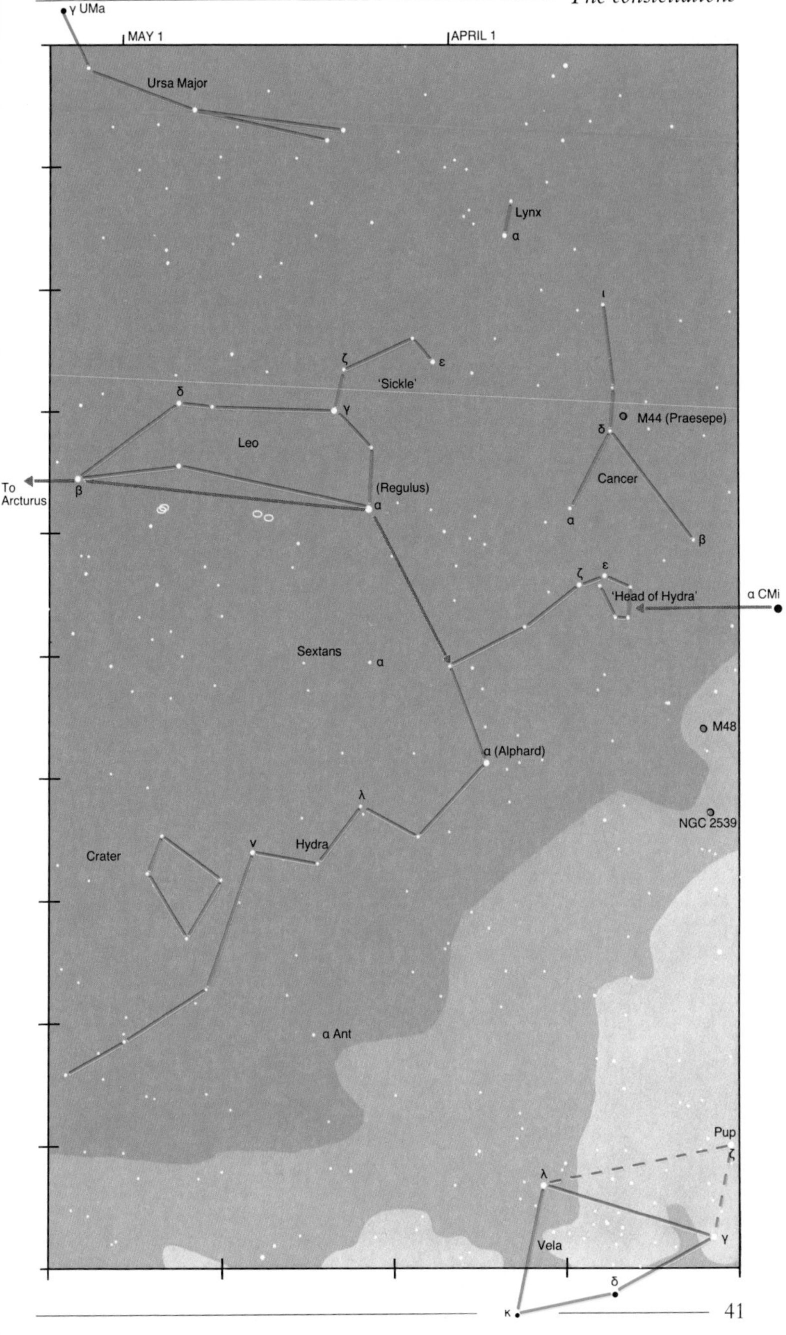

γ UMa

MAY 1

APRIL 1

Ursa Major

Lynx
α

ι

ζ
ε
'Sickle'

δ
γ

M44 (Praesepe)
δ

Leo

Cancer

To
Arcturus
β

α (Regulus)

α

β

ζ ε
'Head of Hydra'
α CMi

Sextans
α

M48

α (Alphard)

NGC 2539

λ

Crater
ν Hydra

α Ant

Pup
ξ

λ

γ

Vela
δ

κ

Equatorial constellations
May, June, July

If you continue the curve of the 'tail' of Ursa Major round and down towards the equator for approximately 30°, you arrive at Arcturus, α Boo (magnitude 0·0), the fourth brightest star in the sky after Sirius, Canopus, and α Centauri, all of which are in the southern hemisphere. Boötes (Boo) is fairly distinct as a 'P'-shaped group of fairly bright stars, north and east of Arcturus. The brightest of these, Izar (ε Boo) is a well-known double star.

The same arc in the sky leads on from Arcturus to Spica (α Virginis) just south of the ecliptic, and beyond that to the four main stars of Corvus. Virgo (Vir) is a large constellation on both sides of the equator, but with no stars other than Spica brighter than magnitude 3. Almost due south of Denebola in Leo lies β Vir, and the constellation can be traced in rough quadrilaterals of third- and fourth-magnitude stars eastwards below Arcturus.

The constellation of Libra (Lib), once the 'claws' of Scorpius (Sco) to the east, is about as far south as Spica. The brightest star (β Lib) forms a triangle with Spica and Arcturus to the west. The fainter, third-magnitude α Lib is almost exactly on the ecliptic slightly farther to the southwest.

In the north, the single bright star of the small constellation of Canes Venatici (CVn) is isolated in the centre of the arc formed by the 'tail' of Ursa Major. To the south lies the faint constellation of Coma Berenices (Com), which like Virgo contains many distant galaxies.

To the east of Boötes is the almost perfect circlet of stars forming Corona Borealis (CrB). This attractive constellation contains first-magnitude Gemma (α CrB) and the important variable R Coronae Borealis. The straggling line of stars forming Serpens Caput, half of the constellation of Serpens, leads down towards the south.

North of Crux and the two bright stars α and β Centauri are the remaining bright stars of Centaurus, forming a rough pentagon south of the 'tail' of Hydra, which has only two fairly bright stars in this region, although the variable R Hya sometimes rises to a little below 4th magnitude. One of the brightest 'stars' in this part of Centaurus is, of course, the magnificent globular cluster ω Centauri – the finest in the whole sky. To the east of Centaurus lies the irregular, but very approximately rectangular constellation of Lupus. Lupus is not very striking as its brightest stars are only about magnitude 3. It runs roughly southwest to northeast towards brilliant, red Antares (α Sco), which is usually a conspicuous object in this area of the sky.

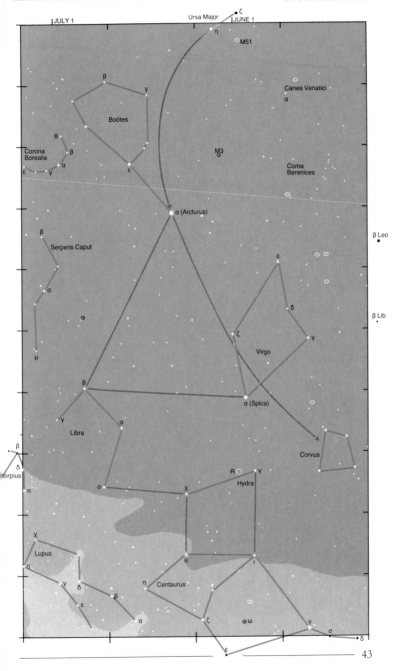

Equatorial constellations
July, August, September

This is the region dominated by the (northern) 'Summer Triangle' formed by Vega (α Lyrae), Deneb (α Cygni), and Altair (α Aquilae) in the north and the stars of Scorpius (Sco) and Sagittarius (Sgr) in the south. It also contains some of the most striking parts of the Milky Way, especially in the south. The large cross formed by the stars of Cygnus (Cyg) is very distinct, its main arm from Deneb to Albireo (β Cyg, a fine telescopic double), pointing south along the 'Great Rift' in the Milky Way (page 182). The roughly 'T'-shaped constellation of Aquila is to the south of the Rift, and also lies across the equator.

The small constellation of Lyra (Lyr) mainly consists of Vega and a small parallelogram of stars to the southeast. Slightly north and east of Vega itself is ε Lyr, the famous 'double double', a wide pair of stars distinguishable to good eyesight, each of which proves to be double in a telescope.

Between Lyra and Corona Borealis to the west are the four stars of the 'Keystone', part of Hercules (Her), with 'arms' and 'legs' stretching out from each corner. Between the two western stars of the 'Keystone' lies the globular cluster M13 (page 181) which is visible as a hazy spot to the naked eye.

None of the stars in Hercules is very bright, only α Her (Ras Algethi) marking the 'head' in the south is about third magnitude. It is a double, one star of which is variable, and lies close to the brighter star α Ophiuchi (Ras Alhague).

The constellation of Ophiuchus (Oph) – the ancient 'Serpent Bearer' – sprawls across both the equator and the ecliptic in a rough pentagon. It divides the two chains of stars that form the halves of Serpens (Ser): the 'head' (Serpens Caput) in the west, and the 'tail' (Serpens Cauda) in the east.

The 'body' of Scorpius (Sco), with red Antares (α Sco) is prominent in the south, with the long chain of bright stars of the 'tail' stretching into the Milky Way. The 'claws' of the scorpion have now been formed into the independent constellation of Libra to the west.

The main portion of Sagittarius also lies in the Milky Way, east of Antares – in fact the centre of the Galaxy (page 185) is here – but the constellation is ill-defined, except for the central region, which has come in recent years to be known as the 'Teapot'. To the south lies Corona Australis, not so bright or easy to see as Corona Borealis. The much fainter constellation of Telescopium is still farther to the south.

The indistinct constellation of Scutum, with the 'Wild Duck' cluster (M11) lies in the heart of the Milky Way between Sagittarius and Aquila. Still farther north, between Aquila and Cygnus are tiny Sagitta and the larger Vulpecula. To the east lies the distinct, small group of Delphinus.

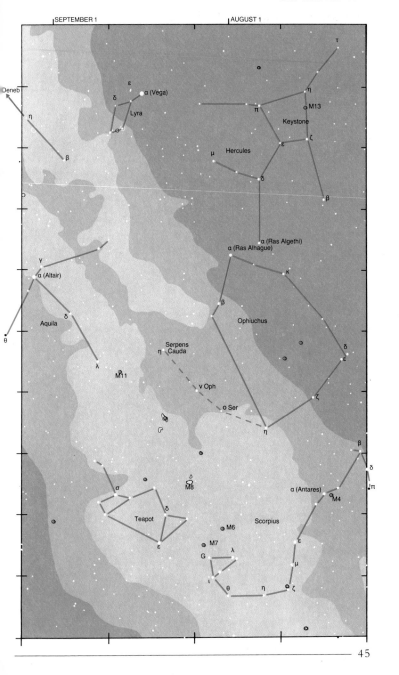

Equatorial constellations
September, October, November

The southeastern 'wing' of Cygnus leads on to Markab (α Pegasi) one of the four stars marking the prominent 'Great Square of Pegasus', which is actually a slightly lopsided rectangle, the shorter sides running almost due north and south. (Continuing the line of the 'Pointers' in Ursa Major right across the pole actually brings you down the side formed by β and α Pegasi.) However, as the star at the northeastern corner is α Andromedae (Alpheratz) only the other three truly belong to Pegasus (Peg). One other bright star (ε Peg) lies roughly half-way between α Peg and Altair. Between ε and the Milky Way are the tiny constellations of Equuleus, and the much more distinctive Delphinus.

The constellation of Pisces (Psc) is supposed to represent a pair of fish joined by a cord, and lies south and east of Pegasus. The little circlet of the western 'fish' is just north of the equator. Much farther north between Cygnus and Cassiopeia, the small zig-zag constellation of Lacerta crosses the visible boundary of the Milky Way.

The continuation of a line from β Cyg (Albireo) in Cygnus (Cyg) to Altair takes you to α Cap, a fairly faint (magnitude 4) visual double, and on to slightly brighter β Cap. Capricornus (Cap) and the next constellation to the east, Aquarius (Aqr) both consist of stars with no very apparent pattern. The only prominent line runs from β Cap, through β and α Aqr, with 'branches' at roughly right angles to δ Cap and ε Peg. Most of the fainter stars of Capricornus lie south of β and δ Cap. To the east of α Aqr there is a small, distinct 'Y'-shaped group of stars, frequently known as the 'Water Jar' – from the time when the constellation was regarded as representing a man carrying water – or more simply as 'the Y of Aquarius'. To the south and east of α Aqr an irregular line of faint stars completes the constellation.

Farther south is bright Fomalhaut (α Piscis Austrini) which forms the 'tail' of a quadrilateral 'kite' marked by the stars γ, α and β Gruis, the two latter stars being more or less in line with α Indi to the west. Between this star and the southern part of Capricornus lies the small and very inconspicuous constellation of Microscopium, only two stars of which, γ and ε Mic, are slightly brighter than magnitude 5. Another faint, but rather larger constellation, Sculptor, lies east of Fomalhaut. Here only α Scl, outside the chart area to the east, is just brighter than magnitude 4·5.

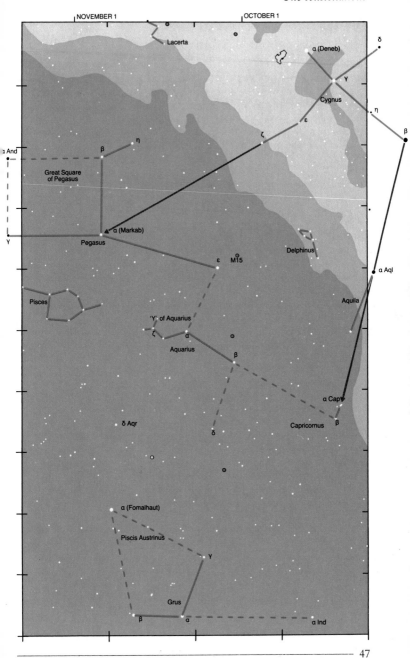

Equatorial constellations
November, December, January

Running northeast from the top of the Square of Pegasus is a prominent line of bright stars formed by the 'body' of Andromeda (And) α, β and γ And, together with α Per, and (with a rather greater gap) α Aur (Capella). At β And a side branch of two fainter stars points up towards Cassiopeia, the second star ν And, lying close to the Andromeda Galaxy, M31 (page 185), a distinctly hazy patch of light to the naked eye. Farther south, in Triangulum, M33, another giant spiral galaxy (page 186), is reputed to be visible to the naked eye under very dark skies and favourable seeing. It can be seen in good binoculars, but its fairly large size and moderately low surface brightness – when compared with M31 – mean that it may be a difficult object for small refractors.

Perseus (Per) has no easily-described shape. One line of stars runs from δ northwestwards past α, γ and on to η Per. Halfway between this last star and δ Cas is the famous Double Cluster, h and χ Per: two star clusters that are visible to the naked eye. From α Per a short line runs south by east to Algol (β Per), a very famous eclipsing variable (page 173), and on to ρ, also variable. To the east a line of stars generally trending south begins at δ Per and ends at third-magnitude ζ, above the Pleiades cluster (page 180).

Two small constellations lie southeast of β and γ And: Triangulum (Tri) and with rather brighter stars, Aries (Ari). The eastern 'fish' of Pisces (Psc) is just a faint chain of stars running southeast from near δ And to fourth-magnitude α Psc (Alrisha) just north of the equator. A little farther and south of the equator is Mira (ο Ceti), another important variable star (page 173) which occasionally may become as bright as the third magnitude, although is more usually about fourth at maximum. The eastern side of the Square of Pegasus points roughly in the direction of the triangular 'head' of Cetus and second-magnitude β. North of the equator, third-magnitude α and a few fourth-magnitude stars form the 'tail' of the sea-monster, Cetus.

In the south the most conspicuous stars are in Phoenix (Phe): α, β, and γ Phe, and third-magnitude 41, θ and χ Eri, with bright Achernar (α Eri) even closer to the south pole. Between these constellations and Cetus are the undistinguished groups of Sculptor and Fornax. The latter largely consists of a triangle of stars of magnitudes 4 and 4·5, lying in a 'bend' of the 'river' forming Eridanus. Running almost parallel to the southernmost portion of Eridanus, and to its southwest, is the long, very inconspicuous constellation of Horologium, only α Hor, at the northeastern end, exceeding magnitude 4.

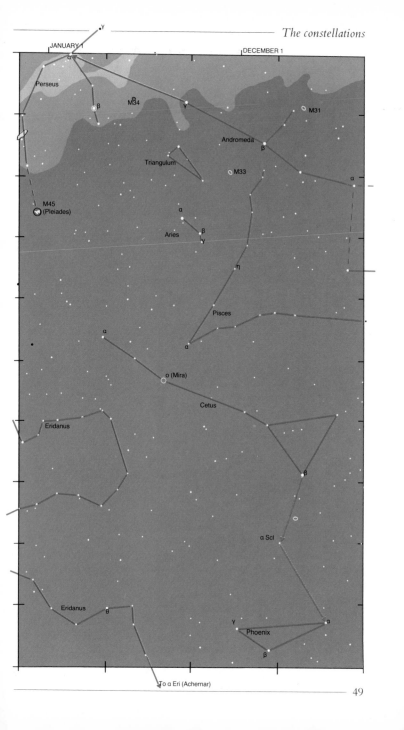

JANUARY 1

DECEMBER 1

Perseus

M34

β

γ

M31

Andromeda

β

α

Triangulum

M33

M45 (Pleiades)

α

β

γ

Aries

η

Pisces

α

α

o (Mira)

Cetus

Eridanus

β

α Scl

Eridanus

θ

γ

Phoenix

α

β

To α Eri (Achernar)

The southern polar constellations

Observers in the southern hemisphere may have no distinct pole star to guide them but many bright groups and individual stars are circumpolar, or very nearly so, as is a considerable portion of the Milky Way, and the two Magellanic Clouds.

The three first-magnitude, and two third-magnitude stars of Crux, often commonly known as the 'Southern Cross', are very distinctive. The dark nebula called the 'Coalsack' is nearby. Beginners (and northerners) should beware of the larger 'False Cross' of second-magnitude stars situated farther along the Milky Way. This consists of the four stars δ and κ Velorum, ι and ε Carinae, rising about three to four hours earlier than Crux itself.

The 'upright' of Crux (Cru) points very approximately towards the south pole, but a line from β Cru across to the centre of the Small Magellanic Cloud (SMC) comes even closer, passing through the third- and fourth-magnitude group of Musca close to Crux. The line from the pole to the Small Magellanic Cloud also forms the base of an isosceles triangle with the central region of the Large Magellanic Cloud (LMC) at its apex.

Rising later than Crux is the brilliant pair α and β Cen (β Cen being the nearer to Crux), which are unmistakable. Follow a line northwest from β, past second-magnitude ε Cen, to locate ω Centauri, a fine globular cluster, about 18° from β Cen. From here a line of stars belonging to Centaurus (Cen) partially encircles Crux on its northern side. The irregular pentagonal shape made by the remaining stars of Centaurus lies still farther north.

Beyond (and south) of α and β Cen is the constellation of Triangulum Australe (TrA), brighter and larger than its northern counterpart. The faint constellation of Circinus (Cir) lies in between, but only α Cir is as bright as magnitude 3. Between Triangulum Australe and the curve of the 'tail' of Scorpius the constellation of Ara also consists of third-magnitude stars.

Although many of the constellations in this area have few bright stars perhaps the most notable figure is the slightly irregular rectangle with one 'Alpha' star from different constellations at each corner: α Pavonis, α Indi, α Gruis and α Tucanae. The third-magnitude star β Indi lies between two of the stars on one side, and β Gruis on an extension of the one opposite. Rising later is the triangle formed by α, β and γ Pheonicis (page 48).

Tucana (Tuc) itself contains the Small Magellanic Cloud (SMC), and the bright, naked-eye, globular cluster 47 Tuc. The SMC lies on a line between bright Achernar (α Eri) and β Hydri, closer to the pole. Hydrus (Hyi) largely consists of a triangle of third-magnitude stars pointing north, with the apex close to Achernar. Another line of moderately bright stars running north is that formed by γ Hyi, α Reticuli and α Doradus.

Round beyond the Large Magellanic Cloud (LMC) we return to the stars of Carina (Car), particularly Canopus (α Car) and those belonging to the False Cross, to the south of which lies second-magnitude β Car (Miaplacidus). The shorter 'cross-bar' points to γ Velorum, while two of the stars δ and κ, are also part of the brightest region of Vela, as mentioned before (page 40).

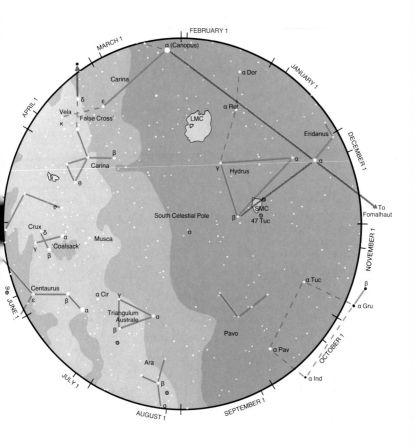

Objects other than stars – what might they be?

It is not uncommon to see something that cannot be identified immediately. Members of the public, unaccustomed to observing, tend to assume that any 'light in the sky' that is not the Sun, Moon or a star, must be an 'Unidentified Flying Object', especially if it moves, flashes or changes colour. Astronomers know that there is a surprisingly large number of ways in which even they may be momentarily confused, but that observation, and a little thought, usually enables the cause to be established.

Even when you know a constellation well, it is easy to forget (or even not to realize) that there is a star in a particular position. Variable stars (page 173), including rare novae, can sometimes make identification difficult. Planets (page 145), can certainly confuse, but they are always close to the ecliptic, and usually appear somewhat steadier than stars, even to the naked eye. Aircraft can be very bright if they are using landing lights, and may seem motionless for quite a while when they are heading towards you. Meteorological balloons can catch the light around dawn and dusk, but usually appear dark against the sky. If watched for a short while they will be seen to move.

Sometimes an individual star seems to move slightly. This can be due to scintillation (page 17) but is most frequently a form of optical illusion which happens to everyone. Many objects do move, of course, the planets slowly, the Moon somewhat faster (page 54). Minor planets (page 158) may move fairly

Below: *A satellite re-entering the atmosphere can appear very similar to a bright natural fireball.*

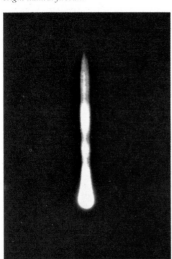

What might it be?

Flashing lights
Colour changes
Fleeting, pin-points of light
Steady, unrecognized points of light
Patches of light
Visible motion
Motion over days (or longer)
Slightly meandering path (satellites)
Waving changes in position (stars)

rapidly if they are close to the Earth, but are usually slow, changing position from night to night. Balloons, aircraft (which usually show coloured and flashing lights), and satellites come next, although with all of these their apparent speed varies greatly with distance and altitude. Artificial satellites (page 120) travel slowly in comparison with meteors and fireballs (pages 113-19), although it does depend on the altitude of their orbit (geostationary satellites are a special case). The slow speed largely distinguishes a satellite re-entry (page 121) from a fireball. In addition satellites frequently disappear into (and appear from) the Earth's shadow. Finally it must not be forgotten that there are many night-flying birds – a low, fast-moving bird, dimly illuminated by light from the ground, has been known to appear strikingly like a faint meteor.

A hazy patch could be one of several things, depending upon its size. The zodiacal light (page 108) can be seen only along the ecliptic over the eastern or western horizons. Auroral patches (page 110), especially at the start of a display, may be taken for clouds illuminated by distant lights. True noctilucent clouds (page 112) have a very distinct appearance and appear only around midnight. Rocket launches and releases of material for upper atmosphere research may give rise to coloured glows which could be mistaken for aurorae (or clouds). In binoculars or telescopes, small hazy patches are usually unresolved clusters and nebulae or galaxies as comets are fairly rare.

The usual cause of strong colour changes in stars is scintillation (page 17), and occurs especially when they are close to the horizon. Refraction (page 13) can produce coloured fringes on one side of planetary disks, and once again this happens when these are at low altitudes.

Aircraft, stars and planets with strong scintillation, tumbling satellites
Aircraft, stars and planets with strong scintillation
Head-on meteors (very rare), effects of vision
Stars, planets, minor planets, variable stars, novae (rare)
Clouds, aurorae, upper-atmosphere experiments, rocket exhaust trails, comets, clusters, galaxies
Birds, aircraft, balloons, satellites, meteors, fireballs
Planets, minor planets, comets
Effects of vision
Scintillation, effects of vision

The motion of the Moon and planets

Obviously any observer in the equatorial zone is in an excellent position to observe the Moon and planets because at times they may pass directly overhead. However, for observers at other latitudes, their visibility is strongly affected by the season. In summer, when the Sun is high, the region of the Zodiac opposite the Sun in the sky must be lowest, and thus be badly placed for observation. In winter the opposite is true. The inclinations of the individual orbits to that of the ecliptic mean that each body may be north or south of the path of the Sun. Due to the brightness of the Moon, and its range in elevation of about 10°, its change in altitude is frequently apparent to even the most casual observer. Its continuous motion eastwards against the stars (by about its own apparent diameter every hour) is not very obvious to the naked eye, but is easily seen with a small telescope.

Left: *Venus photographed on 1980 June 12 when it was nearly at inferior conjunction and only 4·5° from the Sun.*

When any object is on the opposite side of the sky to the Sun it is at **opposition** and is then best placed for observation. This cannot occur with the inner planets Mercury and Venus, so that their observation is easiest at eastern or western **elongation**, when they appear most distant from the Sun. As seen from the Earth, all the planets normally exhibit **direct motion**, slowly shifting eastwards against the background stars. However, because of the relative motions and positions of the planets and the Earth, at times they reach stationary points and then reverse direction. Movement westwards in the sky is known as **retrograde motion**. The reversals occur at eastern and western elongations in the case of Mercury and Venus, and on either side of opposition for the remaining planets. Depending on the actual relative positions of the Earth and the planet concerned, the apparent paths may be open ('S'- or 'Z'-shaped) or closed loops. Similar effects occur, of course, with minor planets and comets.

Nearly all the planets rotate on their axes in the same way as the Earth itself (anticlockwise when looking down on the north pole). Only Venus (page 152) and, strictly speaking, Uranus (page 166) are exceptions. All the planets, and most of the other bodies in the solar system have orbits that also follow this same direct rotation. It is only some comets and planetary satellites that have retrograde orbits, and move in the opposite direction.

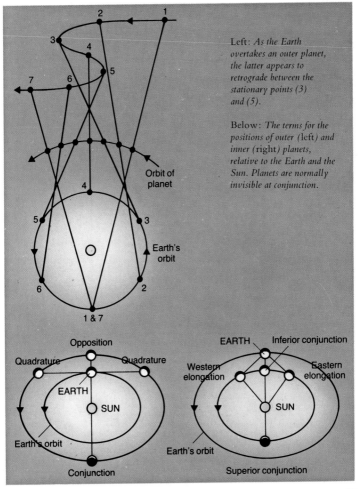

Left: As the Earth overtakes an outer planet, the latter appears to retrograde between the stationary points (3) and (5).

Below: The terms for the positions of outer (left) and inner (right) planets, relative to the Earth and the Sun. Planets are normally invisible at conjunction.

Orbit of planet

Earth's orbit

As all the bodies in the Solar System (including the Earth) orbit the Sun in ellipses, they approach and recede from it. The point on an orbit closest to the Sun is known as **perihelion**, and the most distant, **aphelion**. A planetary disk will naturally appear largest when the distance between the Earth and the planet is least. This effect is particularly important in the case of Mars when the disk may change very dramatically in size. The most favourable oppositions occur when Earth is close to aphelion, and Mars to perihelion. This can only happen in August or September, when the planet is south of the ecliptic, so southern hemisphere observers are permanently favoured in this respect.

The period when a planet is visible is often termed an apparition. It naturally extends on either side of opposition or elongation. Some dates of oppositions and elongations, and approximate positions of the planets for a number of years are given in tables in the individual sections where their observation is described. A table of precise positions, expressed in celestial co-ordinates (page 77), is known as an **ephemeris**. Such tables are generally given in the astronomical yearbooks for each of the major planets.

Binoculars

Binoculars are more useful to beginners than small telescopes, quite apart from being cheaper, and useful for other activities. Their images are the 'right way up', and easier to compare with the naked-eye view or star charts than the inverted fields (page 72) given by telescopes and the majority of finders. Even the most advanced astronomers frequently use them, and there are some observing programmes where other instruments are very rarely employed. The wide field and low magnification make them ideal for observing many star clusters and for general sweeping of the Milky Way, as well as being of use (for example) in tracing the tails of comets when these are too faint for the naked eye, yet too indistinct for larger telescopes and high magnifications.

Choosing binoculars

The old-fashioned opera-glasses, with their very low magnifications, can be helpful on occasions if they happen to be to hand, and are quite useful for scanning the Milky Way. However, do not consider buying them if you wish to do serious observing. Prismatic binoculars are far more satisfactory, but several factors (apart from cost) must be considered. The most important of these are magnification and aperture (the latter always being given in mm), usually engraved in that order somewhere on the binoculars themselves, as '8 × 40' or '7 × 50', for example.

For most general purposes apertures of 40-50 mm are adequate, although of course, the larger the aperture the fainter the objects that can be seen (page 77). Binoculars with apertures larger than 50 mm are certainly desirable for many types of observing, but they are much heavier, and must have some form of mounting to keep them steady.

In the dark the pupil of the eye is generally about 7-8 mm in diameter. In any instrument, the **exit pupil** (the diameter of the bundle of rays leaving the eyepiece) must not be greater than this amount, otherwise light gathered by the objective is being wasted. Occasionally binoculars are offered for sale with low magnification and an exit pupil greater than 8 mm. Check this by dividing the aperture by the magnification; 7 × 50 binoculars, for example, have an exit pupil slightly greater than 7 mm, which is acceptable. If it is less than about 5 mm, the binoculars have a fairly high magnification, would certainly need a support, and are really more suitable for daytime use. If the magnification is unknown measure it by the methods given elsewhere (page 72), which also determine the field of view. In most low-magnification binoculars the latter lies in the range of 5-7°.

Objects for binocular observation

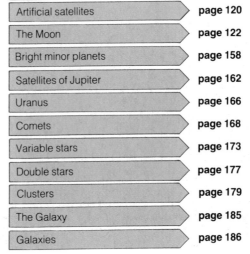

Artificial satellites	**page 120**
The Moon	**page 122**
Bright minor planets	**page 158**
Satellites of Jupiter	**page 162**
Uranus	**page 166**
Comets	**page 168**
Variable stars	**page 173**
Double stars	**page 177**
Clusters	**page 179**
The Galaxy	**page 185**
Galaxies	**page 186**

Left: *Comparison of the size of images obtained by the naked eye and 7x binoculars. The latter are ideal for initial studies as they allow all the major features to be seen.*

High magnifications darken the background and are useful where there is a lot of extraneous light from light pollution, but they narrow the field of view, making it more difficult to find objects in the sky. On the other hand, Jupiter's satellites, double stars, and many clusters are easier to see. However, the most important consideration is that binoculars with high magnifications are difficult to hold by hand. Certainly anything over 10×, and more usually over 8×, requires a proper mounting. (Zoom binoculars with their extra optical elements and consequent light-losses are not worth considering for astronomy.)

Generally more expensive binoculars are of sturdier construction, with more rigid mounting of the prisms, making them less liable to misalignment. Individual focusing of the two eyepieces is more satisfactory, but much rarer, than central focusing. There are at least eight glass/air surfaces in each optical train, so full anti-reflection coating is very desirable.

Left: The globular cluster M15 in Perseus. Binoculars are ideal for locating and observing many similar objects.

Below: The compact design of prismatic binoculars means that they are ideal for many astronomical observations, and can be used anywhere.

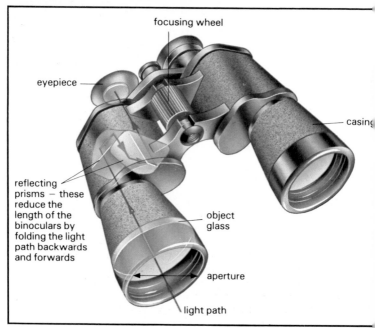

focusing wheel

eyepiece

casing

reflecting prisms — these reduce the length of the binoculars by folding the light path backwards and forwards

object glass

aperture

light path

Testing binoculars

Most tests for telescopes (page 64) may be applied to binoculars, particularly those for chromatic aberration, astigmation, distortion, and flatness of field. Gradually move the binoculars away from your eyes to about 10 cm (4 in) or so. The image should remain single, even if you close your eyes for a moment. At about 30 cm (12 in) the exit pupils should appear perfectly round – showing that the full beam of light is passing through the prisms – and evenly illuminated. The alignment of the two optical systems should be checked; misalignment being a frequent, unrecognized cause of eyestrain and headaches. Check for anti-reflection coatings by viewing, from both eyepiece and objective ends, the images of a light bulb reflected by the optical surfaces; coloured images indicate coated surfaces, and white reflections are returned by those that are uncoated. Very few binoculars are perfect, so don't be too shocked if you find that your old favourites have some faults.

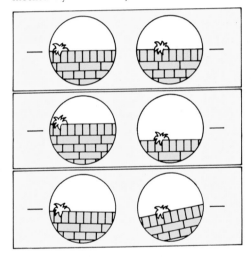

Hold the binoculars away from the eyes and examine a straight-edged object, which should appear perfectly aligned (top). The eyes can compensate fairly easily for vertical misalignment (centre) if it is not excessive, but rotation of one or both images (bottom) can lead to severe eye-strain.

Observing with binoculars

All telescopes perform better if rigidly mounted, but with binoculars the improvement is startling, much fainter detail and lower magnitudes being seen. Any form of support is better than nothing, so try resting them on top of a wall, or pressing them against the trunk of a tree. Adaptors can be made or purchased to fit photographic tripods, but it is usually difficult to use high elevations. Many observers find that an ordinary, reclining, garden chair with arms is very convenient and gives good support for the elbows. However, even further improvement can be obtained from a proper observing seat or stand, mounting the binoculars so that they do not have to be hand-held.

Extraneous light can be a problem, but can be solved by shaped, rubber eyecups, which are well worth fitting in any case. Dewing of the objectives can largely be prevented by dewcaps (page 66), but its occasional occurrence on the eyepieces is difficult to cure.

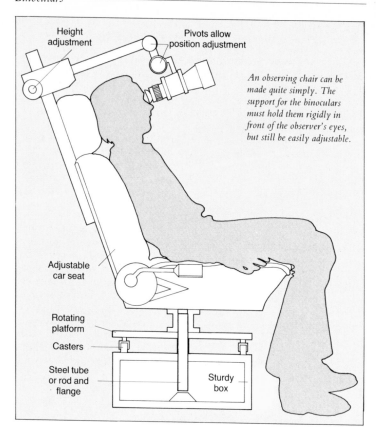

Height adjustment

Pivots allow position adjustment

An observing chair can be made quite simply. The support for the binoculars must hold them rigidly in front of the observer's eyes, but still be easily adjustable.

Adjustable car seat

Rotating platform

Casters

Steel tube or rod and flange

Sturdy box

Binocular objects

CVn	M51	'Whirlpool' – spiral galaxy (faint)
Ori	θ	'Trapezium' – in Orion Nebula
Peg	M15	Globular cluster
Pup	M46	Open cluster
Sco	M4	Globular cluster
Sco	M6	Open cluster
Sco	M7	Open cluster
Sgr	M8	'Lagoon' – diffuse nebula
Scu	M11	'Wild Duck' – open cluster
Tri	M33	Spiral galaxy

Telescopes

In recent years the two traditional types of telescope used by amateurs, the **refractor** which employs a lens (or **object glass**) to form an image, and the **reflector**, which uses a mirror, have been joined by various **catadioptric** forms, using a combination of one or more lenses and mirrors. Whatever the type, the main image-forming element is frequently known as the **objective**, and its aperture (D), focal length (F), and focal ratio (F/D) govern the telescope's main applications. Large apertures with their greater light-grasp are usually desirable, as they also give improved resolution and allow higher magnifications to be used (page 72). For any particular type, however, large apertures are obviously more expensive and less portable than smaller telescopes.

Light-grasp and resolution

The most important factor of any telescope or a pair of binoculars is the **aperture** (D), the diameter of the objective. This controls the light-grasp, which increases as the square of the diameter, dictating the faintest object – the limiting magnitude – that can ever be perceived. A further important quality is **resolution**, the ability to show fine detail, such as planetary markings or double stars (page 177). It is largely dependent upon the size of the objective and a practical value (in seconds of arc) is given by 138/D (the diameter being measured in millimetres). Long focal-ratio objectives (over f/12) may give even better results, closer to 116/D. Partly because of the presence of the central obstruction, reflectors and catadioptric telescopes usually have slightly lower resolutions than refractors of the same diameter. Reflectors, in particular, may also suffer from tube currents, which may greatly degrade the general performance.

Open tubes are most frequently used on large reflectors, such as this 400mm (16″) Newtonian.

Refractors

The object glass (OG) of a refractor is **achromatic**, bringing rays of light of different colours to the same focus. Few amateur refractors operate at focal ratios of less than f/10 or f/12, as achromatic objectives of shorter focal lengths are very expensive. Refractors are therefore best suited to observations requiring long focal ratios, fairly high magnifications, or restricted fields of view (page 72). An aperture of 75 mm is about the minimum for 'serious' observing. Work can be done with smaller sizes but unfortunately most beginners do not appreciate that the small apertures have considerable limitations, and that good binoculars would probably be far more satisfactory. Refractors do not suffer from the central obstructions found in the other types, but 100 mm is near the limit of portability, and the large sizes are very expensive, so that refractors over 150 mm are rare.

Reflectors

Most amateur reflectors operate at focal ratios of f/6 to f/8, and are generally

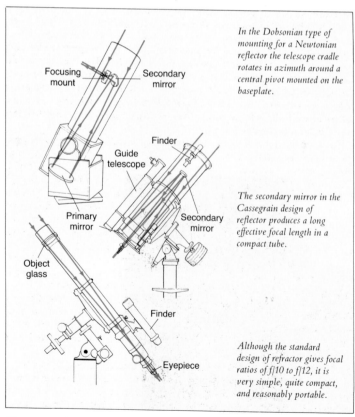

Focusing mount

Secondary mirror

Finder

Guide telescope

Primary mirror

Secondary mirror

Object glass

Finder

Eyepiece

In the Dobsonian type of mounting for a Newtonian reflector the telescope cradle rotates in azimuth around a central pivot mounted on the baseplate.

The secondary mirror in the Cassegrain design of reflector produces a long effective focal length in a compact tube.

Although the standard design of refractor gives focal ratios of f/10 to f/12, it is very simple, quite compact, and reasonably portable.

A 75-mm (3″) achromatic refractor such as this is ideal for the observation of many astronomical objects.

more suitable for wider fields of view and lower magnifications than refractors. The most usual amateur types are the **Newtonian** and the **Cassegrain**. In the Newtonian the secondary mirror is flat, and does not alter the focal length or ratio of the primary. In a Cassegrain the secondary is convex and increases the overall focal length, making it much longer, and thus changes the **effective focal ratio** of the telescope. Cassegrain types therefore have similar uses to refractors.

Reflectors have the big advantage that, aperture for aperture, they are cheaper than any other type. It is also possible to make the required mirrors oneself, or they may be purchased and mounted in a simple, home-built tube. (The housing for optics in a telescope is always known as a 'tube', even though it may have no actual resemblance to one.) When the greatest light-grasp is required, practically all large amateur telescopes (200 mm or more) are reflectors. The smallest useful size for general use is about 150 mm, and this costs about the same as a 75 mm refractor. Such a reflector has a greater light grasp, showing fainter objects, but it is not as portable as a refractor. Some of the smaller–diameter, short focal-ratio reflectors usefully bridge the gap between binoculars and ordinary reflectors. They are also easily portable.

Some disadvantages of reflectors are that occasionally the reflective coatings may have to be renewed, and the optical elements be re-aligned. The two mirrors also need individual dust-covers, which must be removed and replaced carefully whenever the telescope is used, unless an expensive optical window seals the tube. The eyepiece of a Newtonian can assume awkward positions, so a rotating tube is a great advantage.

Reflectors are also subject to tube currents – unless they are sealed with an optical window, when they function like refractors – as the air inside the tube mixes with cooler, outside air. Precautions, such as making the tube oversize and lining it with insulating material can be effective, but it is for this reason that many reflectors have skeleton 'tubes' carrying the optical components. Unfortunately, these may have other problems as they can suffer from air currents caused by warmth from the observer's body – so wear plenty of insulating clothing! – and increased dewing (page 18), which may mean that a proper observatory becomes essential.

A catadioptric telescope, such as this 200 mm (8″), is compact, portable, and suitable for a wide range of observational activities.

Catadioptrics

The **Maksutov** and the **Schmidt-Cassegrain** are the most important of the catadioptric telescopes. They are compact for a given focal length and thus very portable and convenient to use, especially as many designs incorporate drives (page 69) as standard. However they are usually more expensive than refractors or reflectors of the same size. Their focal ratios are generally long (f/10, f/12, or even f/15), so that they are similar to refractors and Cassegrain reflectors in their applications.

Testing telescopes and lenses

Certain optical tests can be carried out by anyone, but it must be remembered that no optical equipment is perfect. The errors, or **aberrations**, must be as small as possible, although the amount which can be tolerated depends upon the type of observations. Planetary and double-star work, and photography, are more demanding than variable-star observation, for example.

A sharp dividing line between light and dark areas, such as the limb of the Moon or Venus, or in daylight the edge of a distant building, should not show any coloured fringes. Reflectors are free from this defect of **chromatic aberration**, but it is usually present, even if only to a very small degree, in other forms of telescope and in binoculars.

Scan across any straight line, or examine a rectangular pattern such as a brick wall to test for **distortion**.

If possible test any astronomical equipment at night on stellar images, although daytime tests on a distant 'artificial star' (such as sunlight reflected from a ball-bearing) will prove useful. Good equipment brings such images to a sharp focus, which under proper conditions appears as a truly circular **diffraction disk**. This should remain circular inside and outside focus; any elongation indicates either **astigmatism**, or possibly that the optical elements are under strain. If a stellar image does not remain sharply focused from centre to edge, **curvature of field** is indicated. It is present in most telescopes, but is normally only a problem when they are to be used for photography. Another defect is **coma**, which is an elongation of images in comet-like shapes at the edge of the field. This is also common, although generally it is more visible in reflectors than in refractors.

Testing the mechanical aspects of telescopes and mountings (page 67) largely calls for common sense. Rigidity is essential, both in the actual

Left: *For densely crowded star fields like this one near δ and β Centauri high magnifications and long exposures make high demands on optical quality.*

Below: *Optical aberrations in any equipment may cause off-axis images to be very strangely shaped, as shown here (in extreme form) by an aerial lens.*

telescope tube and in the mounting itself, where it is best achieved by sturdy axes each with two well-spaced bearings. Thin, spidery designs which are prone to vibration are to be avoided. The rotation on the axes must be smooth, and on equatorial mountings, both axes should be provided with clamps. All drives must function without backlash, as should focusing mounts and other movements. Finders (page 70) and guide telescopes (page 102), and the mounting itself, must be capable of fine adjustment (and locking) to permit accurate alignment.

Using telescopes

Any telescope that has been stored indoors will take 15-30 minutes to stabilize at the outside temperature. During this time the performance will be poor. Reflectors with thick primary mirrors may take much longer to cool down, but if the optics have been well made the main effect may only be that slight refocusing is required. This causes minimal inconvenience when observing visually, but long-exposure photography should not be attempted until equilibrium temperature has been reached.

Dewcaps are simple and save a lot of trouble, but are often forgotten. They are needed on refractors and catadioptric telescopes (and even on some binoculars), and can be made from any suitable insulating material. A dewcap must extend well beyond the objective, like a lens hood, but must not interfere with the edges of the field of view.

This photograph of Mars, taken with an amateur-sized catadioptric telescope, shows what can be achieved with careful attention to equipment and techniques.

It is most important to try to keep all the optical surfaces clean. A well-fitting dust cover should be used over the object glass of a refractor, or the open end of a reflector's tube. In addition reflectors usually require individual covers over the two mirrors. No covers should be installed until any dew has evaporated completely from the optical surfaces. If possible, a box should be made that will take the whole telescope, but usually this is only feasible for refractors and the catadioptric types. Eyepieces should be removed and stored in a box with a tight lid, giving protection against dust, together with any other small accessories. Although it is often omitted, the focusing mount should also have a cap, to prevent the entry of both dust and spiders. Avoid touching any optical surfaces with the fingers.

If these precautions are taken it should only rarely become necessary to clean the optical surfaces. This might be required perhaps once a year. Remember, however, that scratches are the worst form of damage to any optical surface, and that even visible dust and slight smears will produce little optical effect. Cleaning should only be undertaken when the condition has started to affect optical performance. Frequent cleaning is likely to do far more harm than good.

Treat the optical parts of telescopes, like photographic lenses, with the utmost care; the reflective coatings on mirrors, and the anti-reflection coatings on lenses are particularly vulnerable. Remove surface dust with a photographic blower, one of the special cans of compressed gas, or by the careful use of a soft-haired (photographic) brush. Never wipe away grit with a cloth or tissue.

If lens surfaces are badly soiled, and they are known to be hard-coated, remove surface dust and then use a photographic, lens-cleaning fluid, preferably with one of the special cleaning cloths, or else lens tissue. The eye-lenses of eyepieces are particularly prone to becoming smeared, especially if they are not recessed into the mount. Some eventual deterioration is almost inevitable with such surfaces. Cleaning mirror surfaces (apart from the removal of surface dust) is best left to the expert. Even with protective overcoatings, the reflective surfaces do deteriorate, and will have to be replaced by a specialist firm.

Mountings

There are two main types of mounting for telescopes, of which the first, the **altazimuth**, can be simple and cheap. Such a mounting has a horizontal and a vertical axis, which enable it to be moved in altitude and azimuth (page 22). However, with altazimuth telescopes, the orientation of the field of view, and of any finder, alters with the direction in which it is pointed, so location of faint objects may be a problem, especially when charts are being used. Despite this, with experience, quite advanced observing may be undertaken, but photography is impossible.

The other form of mounting, the **equatorial**, has one axis (the polar axis), parallel to that of the Earth, so that the apparent rotation of the stars can be followed without difficulty by a simple rotation at the correct rate (page 99). This is essential for proper photography, and enables setting circles and drives to be fitted (pages 89 and 69), quite apart from being generally more convenient to use.

The first of the two main equatorial mountings is the Fork mounting, which is very rigid, and is normally found on commercial catadioptrics. It is ideal for Newtonian reflectors, as apart from its other advantages, the height of the eyepiece above the ground is kept to a minimum. The other type, the

German mounting, is best suited to refractors or Cassegrain reflectors, as it allows reasonably easy access to the eyepiece. It is a very common, and reasonably satisfactory, design for commercial Newtonian reflectors.

Tripods are frequently used for small telescopes of all types, and are common for small-diameter refractors on both altazimuth and equatorial mounts. They have the great advantage of being portable, and are reasonably successful for fairly large-diameter (150-200 mm) catadioptric telescopes, which, being compact, are reasonably stable. If a tripod has to be removed after each observing session, set location points for each of the legs into the ground, which will enable you to place it in position with the minimum of trouble each time.

In the northern hemisphere it is easy to orientate any portable mounting with sufficient accuracy for all visual, and some photographic work. Locate Polaris in the finder, clamp the telescope in declination, and then rotate it backwards and forwards in RA. Adjust the alignment until the star remains within about 1° of the centre of the finder's field.

In the southern hemisphere the procedure is more difficult, with no bright star close to the pole, but the fainter fifth-magnitude σ Octantis – also within a degree of the pole – can be used in exactly the same way. Long-exposure photographs require more accurate methods of alignment.

Any telescope benefits from a proper rigid, permanent (or semi-permanent) mounting, and this is certainly required for all large refractors and reflectors, but the performance of 'portable' Schmidt-Cassegrain or Maksutov telescopes will also be improved. A metal or concrete pier is very suitable, but must be of an appropriate height for the type of telescope, bearing in mind all the possible

elevations which the eyepiece may assume when in use. It is most important that any permanent mounting should allow the equatorial head to be adjusted in both altitude and azimuth, to align the axis with the celestial poles. Too frequently, this is difficult to carry out. If the telescope and mounting have to be removed and stored elsewhere, fix a locating plate to the top of the pier so that the telescope does not have to be aligned every time it is installed.

Telescope drives

All telescopes, including altazimuths, benefit from being provided with a slow motion on each axis, even if only powered by hand. The final position can be adjusted precisely while looking through the main eyepiece, an equatorial mount allows the polar axis to be driven at sidereal rate to counteract the Earth's rotation. Although all forms of mechanisms have been used, nowadays electrical drives are most common, and are found on both fixed and portable telescopes. Electrical safety is essential, and can be ensured by using low voltages (12-24 V). Little power is required to drive even large telescopes if they are well-balanced, so vehicle batteries are frequently suitable. If line voltage is used an isolating transformer must be incorporated in the power supply.

Many drive units allow the basic rate of rotation to be varied, and this is particularly useful for guiding during long-exposure photographs. Some may also provide lunar or solar rates. Photography is also easier if the declination axis is fitted with a slow-motion drive, enabling corrections to be carried out whilst guiding.

Far left: *This equatorial mounting carries two cameras of 230 mm (9″) and 150 mm (6″) aperture (f/4 and f/6.3, respectively), together with a 75-mm (3″) refractor and 150-mm (6″) reflector used for guiding.*

Centre: *The German mounting is a common form of mounting, suitable for small reflectors (as here), refractors and catadioptric types.*

Left: *A long-focus (f/15) reflector with a 100 mm mirror, specially designed for observation of the Moon with high magnifications.*

Long-exposure photographs, such as this one of the southern globular cluster ω Centauri, require accurate telescope drives and guiding.

Finders

Most telescopes have restricted fields of view and even if provided with setting circles (page 89), require auxiliary wide-field finders to locate objects. The size of the objective glass and the magnification for such a finder are not critical, although, as with binoculars, a diameter of at least 40-50 mm is very desirable. Magnifications and field sizes similar to those of binoculars will be found to be most convenient, and should be measured in the same way (page 72). Try to obtain an image orientation like that of the main telescope. This will make life a lot easier, although elbow finders of the type that have roof or pentagonal prisms, and give erect (rather than inverted) images, are very convenient on reflectors. The altered field orientation given by ordinary diagonals, which may change with the telescope position, can be highly confusing and most frustrating when searching for faint objects in crowded star fields. 'Straight-through' finders, with the option of fitting a diagonal, are best for refractors and catadioptric telescopes, although some of the latter incorporate their own finding systems.

All finders require cross-wires, either single or double, to determine the centre of the field. Some means of adjustment must be provided so that the alignment with the main telescope may be altered, and locked once correct. Simple focusing arrangements may be required if several observers use the telescope.

Dustcaps are advisable, just as with any telescope, and must be completely opaque and well-fitting if the main telescope is to be used for any solar work (page 139).

Eyepieces

Eyepieces magnify the primary image formed by the objective. There are many different designs, and the type to choose depends upon the focal ratio of the objective and the required field of view. Short focal-ratio Newtonian reflectors generally require more highly corrected eyepieces than refractors, catadioptrics, or Cassegrain reflectors, if the aberrations are to be kept under control. For wide fields, types such as the Erfle and König are frequently employed. At moderate magnifications less complex (and therefore cheaper) designs such as the Ramsden, and the Achromatic Ramsden – frequently, but incorrectly, known as the Kellner, a slightly different type – perform well with most telescopes. More complicated forms such as the orthoscopic and Plössl eyepieces give excellent images in a wide range of focal lengths, and are more convenient for those who must wear spectacles. As always, fully-coated optics are desirable to achieve maximum light transmission and maximum contrast.

Left: *This 150-mm (6″) Newtonian on a Dobsonian mount carries a good, 50-mm (2″) finder.*

Below: *The location of faint objects, especially galaxies – this is M81 in Ursa Major – requires a finder that is properly aligned with the main telescope.*

Magnification of eyepieces and telescopes

An eyepiece is always specified by its focal length, and you can find the telescope's overall magnification by dividing the focal length of the objective by this number. A 25-mm eyepiece used with a mirror or lens of 1 metre focal length therefore gives a magnification of 40 times. However, the quoted focal lengths of eyepieces (and telescopes) are frequently incorrect, so it is a good idea to measure the magnification directly. First find the diameter of the exit pupil (page 57) by pointing the telescope at an evenly illuminated surface – the sky will usually do quite well – with an eyepiece in place. Measure the diameter, d, of the illuminated exit pupil, as accurately as possible. Divide this into the clear diameter of the telescope's object glass, or primary mirror. This gives the magnification. This method is easy and provides a reasonably exact value of the combined magnification of the telescope and eyepiece.

It is just as well to determine the field of view of each eyepiece. An approximation is given by 30° divided by the eyepiece's magnification, but it will vary depending upon the type of eyepiece. Check this at night by first locating a star that is as close as possible to the celestial equator – δ Orionis is a favourite one to use. Point the telescope just preceding (page 88) the star,

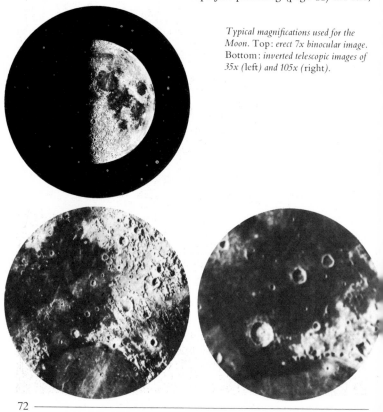

Typical magnifications used for the Moon. Top: erect 7x binocular image. Bottom: inverted telescopic images of 35x (left) and 105x (right).

clamp both axes, and record the time it takes for the star to drift across the diameter of the field. Convert this time to degrees and minutes of arc (table – page 23) to obtain the field of view. For the wide fields of binoculars or finders this procedure is a little tedious, and it is rarely essential to know the field diameters exactly. In this case, find two stars of known separation, which just fit within the field. These can either be two stars on the equator, or two with essentially the same right ascension (page 77), differing only in declination. A cluster with well-determined positions for many bright stars, such as the Pleiades, is ideal for this purpose.

Keep a note of the magnifications and fields of view given by your eyepieces, as this can often be helpful, especially when trying to find difficult objects. It is useful, too, to draw the field of your binoculars or telescope finder to scale on a piece of tracing paper or acetate, so that it can be placed upon your charts.

CHOICE OF MAGNIFICATION As mentioned under binoculars (page 57) the minimum usable magnification gives an exit pupil similar to that of the expanded pupil of the eye – about 8 mm. Consequently, a 150-mm telescope

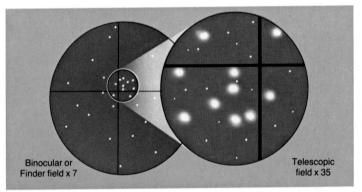

Binocular or
Finder field x 7

Telescopic
field x 35

A comparison of typical magnifications provided by binoculars and a telescope. The latter gives a magnified, inverted image that, depending on the aperture, will show fainter stars.

needs a magnification of about 150/8 (=18·75) as an absolute minimum. In practice greater magnification is normally used, except in very specialized applications such as comet or nova searches, which frequently employ large binoculars in any case.

Choose an eyepiece to provide just the required field of view. Nearly all beginners have a tendency to use too high a magnification, but experience shows that resolution is rarely improved, so that higher magnifications do not necessarily show greater detail. In addition, larger images of extended objects such as planets or nebulae are always dimmer, as the same amount of light is spread over a greater area. In theory the image of a star in a good telescope remains a point, whatever the magnification. In practice this is not always the case, but in variable star work, for example, a higher magnification may be useful to darken the sky background, or to expand a crowded star field.

A good working figure for the normal magnification is approximately the same as the diameter of the objective in millimetres, with the limit being about twice this amount. The higher magnifications can sometimes be used when seeing conditions are exceptionally good. A useful range of eyepieces for a 150 mm, f/6 reflector, or 75 mm, f/12 refractor (both of which have focal lengths of 900 mm) might be 25 (or 24), 18, 12 and 6 mm, giving magnifications of 36, 50, 75 and 150. Depending upon the exact type of eyepiece, these might have fields of about 50, 36, 24 and 12 minutes of arc, respectively.

Left: *Magnification is very critical in planetary observation. Increased magnification of this image of Jupiter would not give better resolution of detail.*

Eyepiece accessories

A **Barlow lens** is a diverging lens which effectively increases the focal length of the objective. It can be useful for increasing the range of a set of eyepieces, or for bringing the prime focus sufficiently far from the telescope for a camera to be used. However, it does not increase the maximum magnification that can be employed, and imposes a penalty in increased light loss, even with full anti-reflection coating. If buying a Barlow, make sure that it does extend the range of all your eyepieces and not merely duplicate the magnifications that you already have.

An attachment which has the opposite effect to that of a Barlow is a **focal reducer** (sometimes called a telecompressor). It has become more common since the introduction of catadioptric telescopes, and when used with them gives a lower effective focal ratio, and consequent faster speed for photographic purposes.

Access to the eyepiece of refractors and Schmidt-Cassegrain telescopes can sometimes be very difficult at high elevations. A **diagonal**, which turns the light path through a right angle, is essential, even though it gives a further light loss, and produces an inversion which can be very inconvenient when making drawings, for example. The type incorporating a pentagonal prism avoids this problem, although usually has greater light loss. Not all focusing mounts allow one to be used, as it needs to be much closer to the objective than a normal diagonal or eyepiece.

Observatories

Although hemispherical domes are the most difficult to construct, they offer the best protection to the telescope and observer.

Any permanently-mounted telescope requires some protection, and this may be little more than a form of shed which divides, or moves out of the way for observing. However, a proper observatory that gives shelter against the wind will protect the telescope from vibration, and keep the observer warmer. It also helps to prevent interference from nearby lights, and can reduce the problems of dewing (page 18). By having everything to hand, and ready to use, more time can be spent observing, rather than transporting equipment backwards and forwards.

The simpler observatories have roofs that lift off, fold back, or slide away to the side, but undoubtedly a dome (not necessarily hemispherical) is best for giving protection against winds and lights. However, as it has to rotate in azimuth, it is far more complicated, and has to have a weatherproof slit which may be opened for observations. All observatories should be opened some time before observing begins, so that the internal and external temperatures have a chance to equalize. This reduces the local air currents that can otherwise help to degrade the seeing (page 16).

The interior of any observatory needs to be uncluttered to avoid bumping into things in the dark, but it will usually be possible to arrange storage space for equipment, and a flat worktop for charts, handbooks, notebooks and other material. An observatory clock (showing Universal Time – see page 90) is essential, as is a permanently-mounted, suitably dim red light for illumination when required.

Star charts

Detailed charts are helpful to any astronomer, and become essential when faint objects must be found. Certain choices have to be made when mapping the sky, particularly the faintest stars to be shown – the limiting magnitude (page 61). As the number of stars increases rapidly towards fainter magnitudes (page 172), the number of map sections required to cover the whole sky rises considerably, if the charts are not to be too crowded and confusing. Towards fainter magnitudes, too, it becomes difficult to be certain that all the stars have been included. So every chart or atlas is a compromise.

Charts and atlases may be prepared showing either white stars on a black background, resembling the night sky, or else reversed, with black dots for the stars. Both types have their advantages. The first (sometimes called 'field' editions) are particularly suitable for use at the telescope when you are seeking very faint objects, as the small amount of white space causes the least loss of dark adaptation of the eyes, which can occur even with a dim red light if large expanses of white paper are examined for any length of time. They are also sometimes better for beginners, who find that the representation closer to the actual appearance of the heavens causes least confusion. However, the majority of charts are black on white, and the big advantage is that you can use them to plot any other objects that may interest you. Many atlases are available in both versions.

The charts given here show stars down to magnitude 5, and are suitable for

most naked-eye work, where the normal limit is about 6 under good conditions. (About forty times as many stars are visible in even moderate-sized binoculars.) Binocular and telescopic charts are much more detailed, but normally only show restricted regions of the sky around specific objects. For faint variable stars, for example (page 173), a series of such finder charts may gradually lead the observer in towards the variable.

Apart from the Greek, and some Roman, letters given by Bayer, objects on charts and in catalogues are identified by various numbers and letters. Some of the designations most commonly encountered are Flamsteed numbers (usually the fainter naked-eye stars), Messier numbers (clusters, nebulae and galaxies), and single or double Roman letters, beginning at 'R' (variable stars).

Celestial co-ordinates

The way in which the major constellations are identified (pages 36–50) and the commonest method of using finder charts can be called 'star-hopping' – using patterns of stars to find the objects wanted. There is nothing wrong with this: it is simple and quick, especially for anyone familiar with the sky. But it is also essential to be able to locate any celestial object precisely, and for this purpose a system of celestial co-ordinates is used. These are **right ascension** and **declination** (abbreviated RA and Dec), which respectively correspond to longitude and latitude on the surface of the Earth.

Part of the brilliant star clouds in the constellation of Scutum.

Right ascension is measured eastwards along the equator in units of time – hours, minutes and seconds. The starting point is the meridian (0^h) passing through the point where the Sun crosses the equator from south to north in March as it travels along the ecliptic (page 25). This point, the vernal equinox, is also known as the **First Point of Aries** (♈), and is as fundamentally important in charting the sky as the Greenwich Meridian is in mapping the Earth.

Declination is measured in degrees and minutes of arc, north ($+$) or south ($-$) of the celestial equator. Celestial co-ordinates can therefore range between 0^h and 24^h ($= 0^h$) in right ascension, and between $+90°$ and $-90°$ in declination.

The co-ordinates of objects may be easily determined from a chart and are usually given in lists and catalogues. For example:

	RA	Dec
Sirius	$06^h 45^m$	$-16° 42'$
Andromeda Galaxy	$00^h 43^m$	$+41° 16'$

For most purposes the stars may be regarded as fixed in RA and Dec. In fact, however, mainly due to the gravitational effects of the Moon and the Sun the Earth's rotational axis is slowly swinging round with respect to the stars. This **precession** causes the right ascension and declination of the stars to change slightly, but continuously, and is the reason that the 'First Point of Aries', once in that constellation, is now in Pisces. To prevent confusion, charts are therefore drawn for specific, fixed dates, such as the beginnings of the years 1900, 1950 or 2000. These are known as Epochs, and are frequently quoted (in parentheses) after listed co-ordinates. For example: α Centauri – $14^h 39 \cdot 6^m$, $-60° 50'$ (2000). The positions quoted here and the charts are for Epoch 2000. For most visual work the changes between Epoch 1950 and Epoch 2000 are not very great, and older charts and catalogues may be used fairly easily.

Catalogue designations

Greek alphabet Roman letters A-Q	Bayer letters	Bright stars
Fl1, Fl2...	Flamsteed numbers	Fainter naked-eye stars
M1, M2, ...	Messier numbers	Brightest clusters, nebulae
NGC 1, NGC 2, ...	NGC numbers	New General Catalogue – clusters, nebulae and galaxies
IC 1, IC 2, ...	IC numbers	Index Catalogue – clusters, nebulae and galaxies
R, S, etc.; RR, RS, etc.; AB, AC, etc.; BB, ... QZ; V355 ...		Variable stars

However, as precession affects the position of the true celestial poles, the changes must be taken into account when aligning telescope mountings for long-exposure photography.

The RA on the meridian for any observer at any particular time is identical to the Local Sidereal Time (page 91). It is frequently convenient to know the **hour angle** (HA) of an object, that is the difference between its RA and that on the meridian. Strictly speaking hour angle is measured westwards (in the same units as RA), as it increases with time, and it may be necessary to add 24h to obtain the correct value. However, it is frequently regarded as applying in either direction, and given as hour angle west, or hour angle east of the meridian.

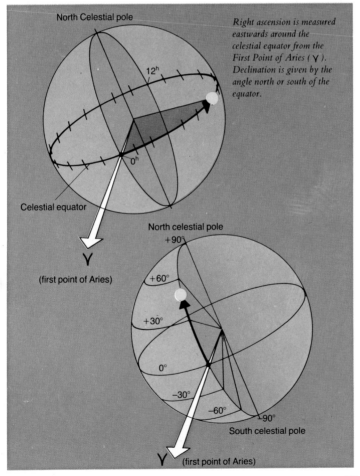

North Celestial pole

Right ascension is measured eastwards around the celestial equator from the First Point of Aries (♈). Declination is given by the angle north or south of the equator.

12ʰ

0ʰ

Celestial equator

♈

(first point of Aries)

North celestial pole
+90°
+60°
+30°
0°
−30°
−60°
−90°
South celestial pole

♈ (first point of Aries)

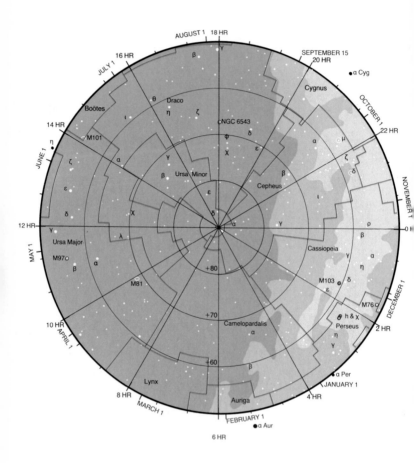

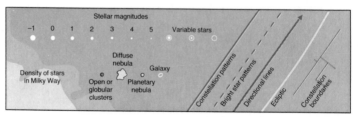

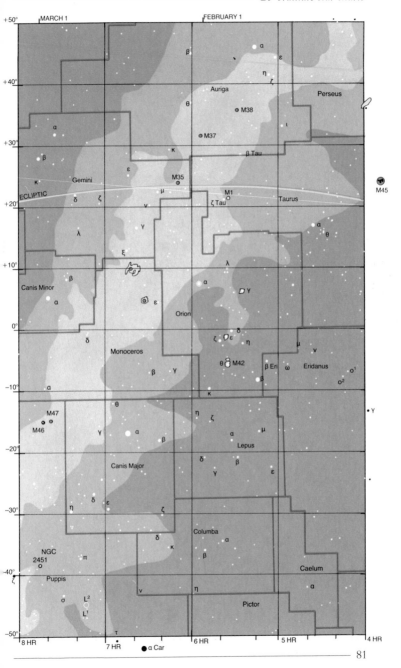

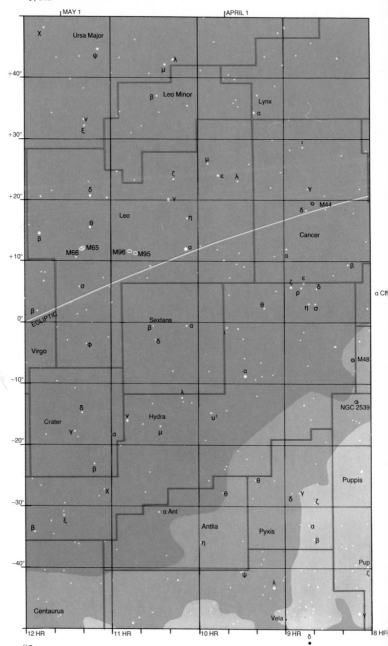

γ UMa

MAY 1 · APRIL 1

Ursa Major
X
ψ
+40°
λ
μ
β Leo Minor
Lynx
ν   α
ξ
+30°

μ
ζ   ε λ   ι
δ   γ   γ
+20°   δ ○ M44
Leo   Cancer
θ   η
β   α
M66 ○ M65   M96 ○○ M95   α   β
σ   ζ ε δ
ECLIPTIC   ρ
β   η σ
0°
Virgo   φ   Sextans   θ
β α
δ
α
−10°
λ
δ   ν Hydra   υ¹
Crater γ   α μ
β
X   θ
−20°   θ   δ γ ζ
ξ
β   α Ant   α Puppis
Antlia   Pyxis β
η
−40°   Pup
ψ   ζ
λ
Centaurus   Vela   γ

12 HR   11 HR   10 HR   9 HR δ   8 HR
82   κ ●

α CM

○ M48

NGC 2539 ○

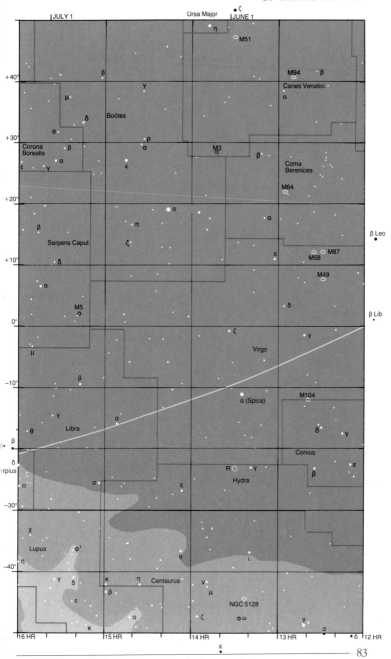

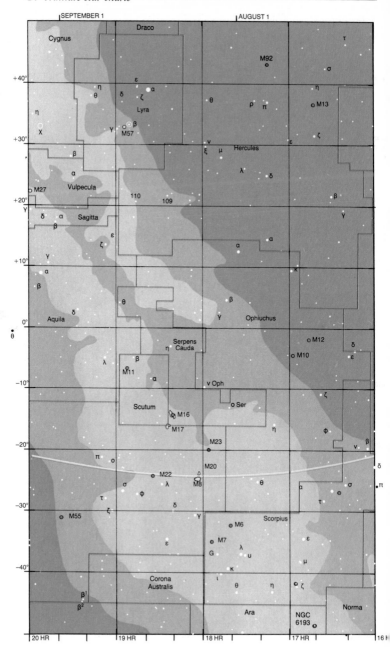

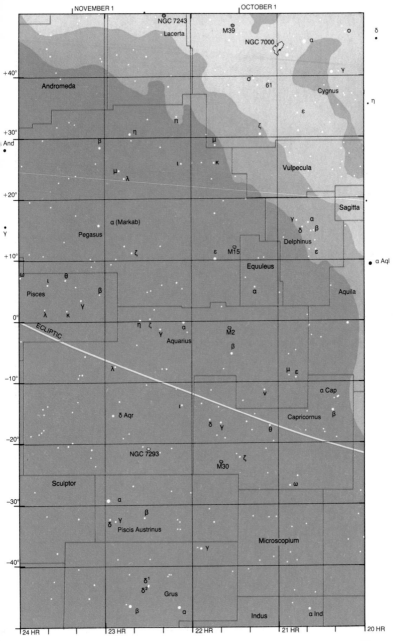

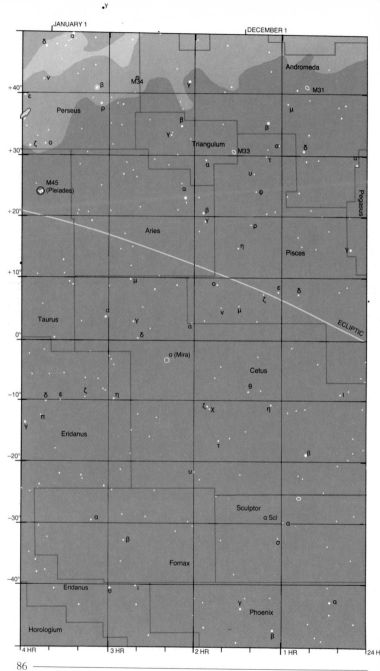

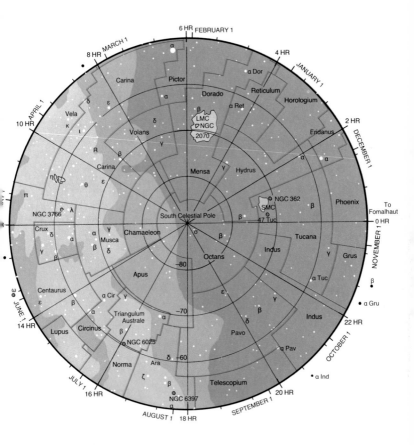

South Celestial Pole

Finding objects with binoculars and telescopes

Comparing charts with the sky can sometimes be very confusing. Binoculars or a telescope usually show more stars than are marked, the apparent scales are different, and the orientation may not be obvious. With regional charts (such as those in this book) turn them to match the sky. Depending upon the equipment with which an object is likely to be observed, finder charts may be prepared with north at the top (for binoculars), or south at top (for telescopes). An inverted field rarely causes great problems, but diagonals (page 70) can give strange reflected or inverted images so that charts have to be viewed from the back against a light. Avoid diagonals, especially on finders, until you are familiar with the field sizes of your telescope and finder.

Looking through an eyepiece it is generally possible to recognize a pattern

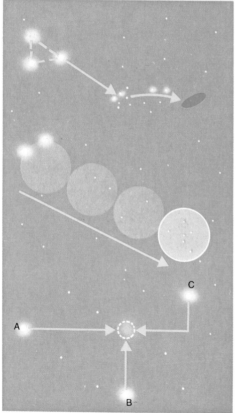

In 'star hopping' (top), the patterns shown by the brighter stars are used as a guide to the position of fainter stars and eventually to the object required. When the field size is known it may be used (centre) to locate faint objects from η brighter, easily visible ones. Bottom: Other useful methods of finding objects are sweeping in RA (A) or Dec. (B), and offsetting in both co-ordinates from stars of known position (C). With an inverted field, the globular cluster is following (east of) star A, due south of star B, and north preceding star C.

of brighter stars somewhere in the vicinity of the object, and charts can be turned if necessary, so that their pattern matches the sky. If you have great difficulty with a telescopic field, perhaps in the crowded regions of the Milky Way, it frequently helps to identify guide stars first with binoculars, then pick up the same stars in the finder. Making a drawing of the field can also help with positive identification.

If you have no chart with which to 'star-hop', you need to know the co-ordinates of any object you want to find. Setting circles – described below – make the job easy, but there are methods that can be used without them. Sometimes positions are given relative to bright stars, using the terms **preceding** and **following;** otherwise calculate the offsets from listed positions. Remember to convert the difference in RA into degrees, then step across from a bright star using the field diameter as a guide. This can be done with any equipment, although it is far easier with an equatorial, when true 'sweeping' can be used. Look up a bright object with the same RA or Dec as the object you want. If the RA is the same, centre the bright star, clamp the RA axis, and sweep north or south in declination. Clamp the other axis if declination is the known co-ordinate, and sweep in RA. If you still have trouble, there is yet another trick you can try. Find something with the same Dec, but preceding the object. Clamp both axes and wait the appropriate amount of time until the Earth's rotation brings the elusive object into the field of view. (You can, of course, do this with an altazimuth mounting, but only on the meridian.)

Setting circles

If a mounting has been properly aligned with the celestial pole, graduated setting circles may be used to point the instrument at any object. These circles should be as large and accurate as possible. A declination circle 150 mm (6 in) in diameter might have degrees and probably 30′ subdivisions, and a similar right ascension circle would have hours, subdivided into 2-minute intervals. Each circle is provided with an index against which a reading is taken. Declination presents little problem, as the circle may be read directly, or else used to offset from an object of known declination. Similar offsetting is possible in the other co-ordinate by simply taking the difference in RA and essentially using the circle as a protractor.

Finding the right ascension directly is slightly more complicated as it involves knowing (or finding) the sidereal time (page 91), and depends upon whether the RA circle is fixed to the polar axis, or is adjustable. Taking the fixed case first, the circle must read 0^h with the telescope pointing due south. Find the hour angle (HA) of the desired object (page 79), and turn the telescope the appropriate amount east or west of the meridian. When the RA circle is adjustable centre a bright star in the telescope and turn the circle until it reads the (known) RA, then clamp it to the axis. Now turn the telescope until the index reads the RA of the wanted object. This arrangement involves adjusting the RA circle for every new object, but is very suitable for small telescopes. Some sophisticated telescope drives turn the RA circle to follow the stars, so that, once set, the telescope's right ascension may be read at any time.

Time

The time used for ordinary civil purposes is a **mean time** (MT) based upon the average length of a solar day. The actual day length varies throughout the year because of two factors: first because the Earth's speed in its orbit is not constant, and second due to the fact that although the Sun appears to move along the ecliptic, the length of day is affected by its changes in RA. The amount which must be added to mean time to give apparent time (as would be shown by the Sun on an ordinary, simple sundial) is known as the **Equation of Time**, or E.

Time based upon the 'fictitious' mean Sun gives a **Local Mean Time** (LMT) varying with longitude around the world. However, ordinary clocks indicate **standard time** based upon various standard **time zones**, although the use of summer time may complicate the issue.

The time used for reporting astronomical observations and used in handbooks and almanacs is **Universal Time** (UT), otherwise known as Greenwich Mean Time (GMT), the standard time at the zero (or Greenwich) meridian. It is reckoned from $0^h - 24^h$, beginning at midnight. As it is the same

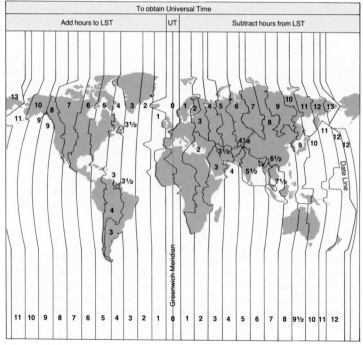

The standard time zones of the world may be used to obtain Universal Time from the observer's local (winter) standard time.

for everyone, everywhere, it avoids a lot of confusion. Every good observatory (and observer) has a clock showing this time. You may obtain UT from your local (winter) standard time by using the diagram.

Another system of time, **sidereal time** (ST) is based on the interval between two successive transits of a star across the same meridian. A sidereal day is approximately 3 minutes and 56 seconds shorter than a mean solar day. Like ordinary mean time, sidereal time is reckoned from $0^h - 24^h$, but it begins when the **vernal equinox**, 'the First Point of Aries' (page 78), crosses the meridian. The **local sidereal time** (LST) is given by the right ascension on the meridian. It can be estimated with a fair degree of accuracy by noting the position of the 'hour hand' on the 24-hour 'clock' around each of the celestial poles. However it is better to establish it exactly. If you observe the transit of a star of known RA across the meridian, you can set an ordinary clock to that time. It will be sufficiently accurate for a single observing session, and can be used for finding objects with setting circles (page 89). However, it is very useful to know your local sidereal time at any particular moment, so see if you can obtain a clock that will run fast by about four minutes per day. Some old-fashioned (i.e. mechanical) clocks can be adjusted by this amount – most battery clocks cannot. Many handbooks give Greenwich Sidereal Time (GST) for 0^h UT. Your longitude (converted to hours, minutes and seconds – table, page 23) gives the difference between your own, individual local mean time and UT, and also – to a sufficient degree of accuracy – between your local sidereal time and Greenwich Sidereal Time.

Dates

To prevent confusion there is an internationally-accepted, scientific way of expressing dates, where the elements are given in the descending order: year, month (in letters, not figures), day, hour, minute, and second (UT). So you might see, for example, 'Middle of lunar eclipse – 1985 May 4, 19:57 UT' (no seconds in this case). Occasionally you may also come across time expressed in **decimal days**, that is in decimals of a day, taken to the required degree of accuracy. (The decimal equivalent of the time just quoted would be 1985 May 4·83125.) This is particularly helpful for carrying out calculations.

It is very convenient to be able to keep track of events which occur a long time apart, such as the appearances of a comet or the maxima of variable stars. The ordinary civil calendar, with its unequal months and leap years is not very suitable. So astronomers often use **Julian days** (JD) for their records. In particular, most variable star observers use JD all the time in reporting observations as it makes the production of light-curves (page 173) so much easier. In this method of calculating the date, the days are numbered from 4713 B.C. January 1 – a time so far in the past that no earlier observations will ever be available. The days start at 12:00 hours (noon) UT, not midnight. Julian day 2,446,067·0 began on 1985 January 1, 12:00 UT, and the total lunar eclipse on 1985 May 4, 19:57 UT is on JD 2,446,190·33125, for example. Tables of JD often give the date for day zero in each month, an apparently strange idea, but which actually makes life easier, because for observations after 12:00 UT you can just add the date. Frequently you only need to use the last few figures of the JD, especially when there is little chance of confusion.

Making detailed observations

It is important to keep a record of your observations – even when you are just starting. Never forget that you could be the only person observing a particular object at a certain time, and that even a rough sketch or just a few details might give information that no-one else can provide. This is one of the reasons why every astronomer is encouraged to submit observations to one of the national or international amateur organizations.

Beginners often feel that their work could not possibly be good enough. This is not true. It is not difficult to make good observations; it merely requires practice for it to become simple and quick. This applies to both 'numerical' observations, such as timing events or making magnitude estimates, and to 'artistic' ones, like planetary drawings. When beginners' observations are compared with those of experienced workers they are often found to agree exactly. Someone's very first variable star estimate for example, has been precisely the same as one made by an observer with many years' experience – the only difference was that the former took much longer to make the observation, and was not so confident of the result.

Keeping records

Have one observing logbook (or possibly one for each main type of object) with fixed pages into which details are entered at the time. (Loose-leaf folders are useful for organizing secondary copies of the main observations.) For each observing session include the date, the time of individual observations, seeing conditions (page 16), and equipment used (telescope, magnification, etc.). As already mentioned (page 91), follow the internationally accepted method for recording dates and times, giving them in the descending order: Year, Month (in letters), Day, and Time (UT). (If for any reason you *have* to use a local or summer time, this *must* be stated in the book.) If the date may change during an observing session, quote the **'Double Date'** at the beginning (e.g. '1985 Aug. 12/13') to prevent confusion.

A drawing of Venus, 1977, February 13, 16:55 UT by Richard McKim, using a 216 mm reflector, magnification 232 times. Seeing II, transparency good.

The actual details recorded will of course depend upon the objects observed, and must be entered at the time. Try to avoid being biased by your own (or other people's) earlier observations. This is not always easy: if you saw a certain pattern of sunspots yesterday, for example, you tend to expect them to be the same when you look today. So record only what you see, not what you think should be there. Never alter details later if they seem wrong, or appear to disagree with anyone else's work. Even very experienced observers make mistakes, and there are always differences between individuals. 'Doctored' observations are worse than useless. If you do spot an error, make a note in your logbook (and on any other copies), so that neither you, nor anyone else will be misled.

Another point worth mentioning is – take your time. Don't rush just because another observer makes several observations whilst you struggle with one. Your one observation may be worth more than all the others. (Of course, some work has to be done quickly, but that is a different matter.)

Venus near inferior conjunction, 1982, January 22, 14:00 UT, by Richard McKim. 200 mm OG, magn 110. Seeing IV, transparency very good. Compare with photograph, p. 54.

How to make drawings

If in doubt, make a drawing. That is good advice for any observer, even those who are not looking at planets or similar objects. If a galaxy, for example, proves to be invisible, make a little sketch in the observing book of the surrounding field. This can show that you were (or were not!) looking in the right place, and helps with identification at a later date. Planetary satellites, minor planets, and similar subjects can be treated in the same way. In any case the concentration required to produce a drawing forces the observer to pay more attention to the object, and usually results in more detail being seen.

Detailed drawing requires some care and patience. It is best to start with something fairly simple, which does not show very intricate detail – as mentioned before (page 26), drawing the naked-eye view of the Moon is quite good initial practice. Planetary disks do not show many features in small telescopes, and are probably easier to draw than a highly-detailed telescopic image of the surface of the Moon. Most whole-disk drawings are made to standard diameters (given later), but other subjects such as portions of the Moon should never be made too large: sizes of 100-150 mm (4-6 inches) square as a maximum. On the other hand, do not cramp yourself for room, and do not attempt to draw too much at once.

Not much is needed in the way of equipment: a clipboard perhaps, some good quality drawing paper, soft pencils (generally 2B and 4B), erasers – the pencil type is useful – and some 'stumps': small pieces of blotting paper rolled into narrow cones. Coloured pencils are excellent for representing Mars, Jupiter and Saturn, and of course, there are many other varieties of medium

Stages in drawing the crater Posidonius (by J. D. Greenwood). A sketch (left) with intensity numbers (page 148) helps with the second drawing. Below (left to right): Beginning with the densest shadows, pencil and erasers build up the finer details.

that may be tried. If ink is to be used, as in lunar work, a denser board may be required, rather than normal drawing paper.

There is no reason why the initial sketches should not be quite rough and carry notes about the position, shape, or intensity of the various features. A 'clean' version may then be prepared later – even away from the telescope. Lay down the broad outlines of the features first, and gradually refine them. The stumps – or your fingers! – may be used to spread out the pencil to give the correct shadings. Use the pointed eraser to pick out small lighter areas. With the Moon, outline drawings of craters are easier for the beginner than trying to reproduce the exact appearance of the highly contrasting features.

A certain amount of work may be carried out away from the telescope, such as using Indian ink to deepen lunar shadows, or Chinese White to pick out brilliant highlights. Ideally however, the finished drawing should be checked against the actual appearance through the telescope. The dark sky background may also be added, usually in black, although blue is sometimes employed for daylight observations of Venus, for example. Again, if ink or colour washes are to be used a heavier board is needed rather than just drawing paper. All pencil drawings should be sprayed with fixative to prevent their being damaged.

If only a few drawings are ever made, glue them into the observing notebook in the appropriate places. (It is best to fix only one edge rather than attempting to paste down the whole of the back, which usually only results in wrinkles.) Make sure however, that all drawings, and most especially those of planets and comets, carry full details, just in case they do ever become detached. If planetary observation becomes your main interest it may be a good idea to choose a notebook (or notebooks for each planet) with fixed, blank leaves of drawing paper. Suitable planetary outlines may be prepared just before starting to observe. Planetary observation is discussed in greater detail later (page 145).

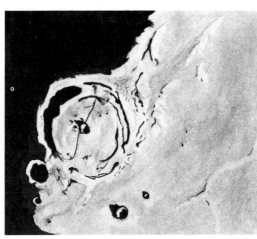

How to take astronomical photographs

There is a fascination in trying to obtain good photographs of celestial objects. Once again, it is not essential for you to have expensive, or complicated equipment to produce satisfactory results. (A few modern, single-lens reflex cameras cannot be used as they rely on battery power to raise the mirror, or keep the shutter open. The batteries can go completely flat in the middle of a single, long, astronomical exposure.) Some types of observational work use quite ordinary, unsophisticated cameras, without any form of special mounting. On the other hand, some amateurs find that faint objects such as distant galaxies pose a great challenge, requiring large telescopes, special films and equipment, and non-standard processing techniques.

Undriven cameras

It is easy to begin by photographing star fields with any ordinary camera that allows time exposures on a fixed mount, such as a photographic tripod. This produces trailed images of the stars, whose length naturally depends upon the exposure, and the distance of the area concerned from the celestial pole, where motion is least. The standard, 50-mm lenses in most 35-mm cameras give fields of about 39 × 26 degrees, which is sufficient to include most individual constellations. With moderately fast colour or black-and-white films (say about 200 ASA), even short exposures of 20 to 30 seconds will show about as many stars as the naked eye, if not more, and the trails will be short. Stars are a very severe test of any optics, and even good-quality lenses can show strangely-shaped images at the edges of the field when used at full aperture. It may be best to use a smaller aperture and as with all other astronomical

Left: *This photograph of Cygnus shows the region of Deneb (α Cyg) and the nearby red glow of the North America Nebula.*

Below: *Photography through a telescope may be supplemented by a simultaneous wide-angle picture using a camera with its own lens.*

This long-exposure photograph, taken looking west, shows straight equatorial star trails and slight curvature farther towards the poles.

photography, this can only be settled by experiment. Similarly, the length of exposure will be partly determined by the brightness of the sky background, whether this is due to artificial lights, or moonlight. If you keep a note of the exposure details, together with the usual information about date and time, this will help you decide what is best for your conditions.

Camera-shake is a problem in any astronomical photography, and a cable, or pneumatic release must be used. The motion of the mirror in single-lens reflex cameras may cause vibration. Some designs allow the mirror to be locked up, and some immediately raise the mirror if the self-timer is used, so the vibrations die away before the shutter is released. If neither feature is available, hold a black card, a black hat or something similar in front of the lens as a simple shutter.

If it is difficult to see faint stars through your camera's viewfinder, make a simple wire-frame to outline the field of view for the standard lens (or lenses). Fix it to the camera, or its mounting plate, and locate the position for your eye by checking the field in daylight. You can use a fixed peep-sight to mark this distance for use in the dark. This device can also be used for driven cameras.

Driven cameras

To avoid trails some form of equatorial mounting is needed, so a camera is frequently mounted on a driven telescope. If this is not available, a simple mounting carrying just a camera is easy to make. The stars can be tracked quite successfully with only a hand drive, so the mount can be fully portable and used anywhere, but like telescope mountings (page 69), electrical drives are frequently used. However, any mount must be aligned reasonably well with the pole (page 67). The longer the focal length of the lens used, and the longer the intended exposure, the more accurately this must be carried out.

Even with a good-quality drive, it is usually necessary for corrections to be made during a long exposure, especially when long focal-length lenses are used. Various errors accumulate and cause the image to wander from the correct position on the film. When the camera is mounted on a large telescope, the latter can be used for guiding. A mounting designed just for cameras can also carry a small, long-focus refractor for this purpose. In both cases guiding can be on any bright star, as the camera and telescope can point to slightly different regions of the sky.

Photography

Fixed camera	Star trails, constellations, meteors, aurorae, noctilucent clouds, artificial satellites sequences or Moon or lunar eclipses
Driven camera (unguided)	Moon, lunar eclipses, constellations, clusters
Driven camera (guided)	Star fields, nebulae, comets (wide-field), minor planets
Telescope + camera & lens	Lunar features
Telescope prime focus	Star fields, nebulae, clusters, comets, galaxies
Eyepiece projection	Planets

Photography through a telescope

Any astronomical photography is greatly affected by the seeing conditions (page 16), but these become particularly important when telescopes and very long exposures are used. The errors caused by atmospheric effects are usually far smaller than those produced by incorrect polar alignment, mechanical problems and faulty guiding (amongst others).

You can obtain photographs by mounting a camera (with its lens) in line with a telescope's eyepiece – both being focused to infinity. However, better results are produced if the light from the telescope is focused directly onto the film in just a camera body or in a specially made film or plate holder. This prime focus photography makes the best use of the available light but the **image scale** is governed by the focal length of the telescope and is approximately given (in mm per degree) by the focal length divided by 57·3. A telescope of 1200 mm focal length (150 mm, f/8 for example) has a prime focus scale of about 21 mm per degree, and a full 35-mm camera frame would cover about 1·7 × 1·1 degrees. This is much greater than any normal, visual field and field curvature is certain to be evident, with out-of-focus images at the edges of the frame. (Photographic lenses are specifically designed to have flat fields.)

Colour photography of the planets is very demanding. This photograph of Jupiter, taken with a 200-mm (8") catadioptric telescope, shows the belts and the Great Red Spot. More detail would be seen visually.

Other aberrations, especially coma in the case of Newtonian reflectors, are likely to be present at the edges of the field. The field becomes flatter and the other aberrations are often reduced as the focal length increases, so changing the effective focal ratio can help.

This can be achieved by using either a Barlow lens (page 74), or **eyepiece projection**, which will also produce a larger image. This is frequently essential in any case – especially with planetary photography. The size of the image of the Moon, which has an angular diameter of about 31 minutes of arc, is about 10·9 mm at the prime focus of a 1200-mm telescope. (The Sun is about the same, but solar photography requires special precautions – see page 140.) The planets with the largest apparent sizes, Venus and Jupiter, can only reach about 60 and 45 seconds of arc respectively. Their sizes would only be about 0·35 and 0·26 mm in diameter, far too small to be enlarged in the darkroom. But any magnification of the image means that it becomes fainter (page 103), requiring a longer exposure with all that this entails.

With a reasonably large-aperture telescope having a long focal ratio, the use of a focal reducer (page 74) can be of considerable help in obtaining photographs of extended objects such as nebulae. The shorter effective focal length and faster focal ratio allow shorter exposures – but the images will be correspondingly smaller, and require more enlargement.

Adaptors are available to couple most interchangeable-lens camera bodies to the drawtubes of focusing mounts. One of the greatest problems with photography through a telescope is obtaining the correct focus. Most focusing screens are unsuitable, as they are designed for use when there is plenty of light. They can be satisfactory with very bright objects, such as the Moon. If you have one of the more expensive cameras with interchangeable screens, you may be able to use the type with a clear centre and engraved crosshairs. With a focusing eyepiece magnifier in place, first make sure that the image of the crosshairs is sharp. This can even be done off the telescope, by pointing the camera, without its lens, towards an evenly illuminated surface – a piece of paper, for example. Do not change the focus of the magnifier afterwards. Looking through the magnifier, adjust the telescope's focusing mount until both the image and the crosshairs appear sharp.

With other cameras it may be necessary to focus at the actual film plane. A focusing plate like the screen mentioned (clear centre and crosshairs) is ideal. (It can be made at home by drawing thin Indian ink lines on a finely ground piece of glass.) Hold the plate on the film plane and focus in the way just described, preferably with a magnifier. Another method is to use a 'knife edge', again at the film plane. With the telescope pointing at a bright star, and the eye held back from the camera, an illuminated circle is visible. With the motion of the star across the knife edge – let the rotation of the sky do this – the image will darken evenly all over, rather than from one side, only when the knife edge is at the precise point of focus. (This is actually a mirror-testing technique known as the 'Foucault Test'.) Obviously both of these methods are more suited to old-fashioned plate cameras than the modern 35-mm variety, and it may be necessary to make up an auxiliary focusing device, holding a screen or knife edge at precisely the distance of the camera's film plane from the end of the telescope's focusing mount.

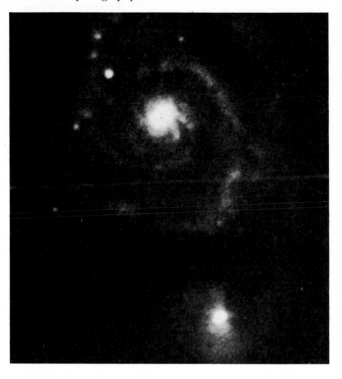

Guiding

The most common method of guiding is by the use of an auxiliary telescope. This is frequently a long-focus refractor mounted on the main telescope. It is helpful if you can adjust it to pick up a bright star outside the main telescope's field if necessary. A guiding eyepiece is needed and this has a set of cross-wires – frequently glass filaments or even spider's web – or occasionally, a reticle engraved on glass. As tracking errors are most apparent at high magnifications, the sky background is dark and cross-wires may not be visible unless some form of faint illumination is provided.

On-axis guiding can be arranged by using a beamsplitter, which may consist of a diagonal coated with a semi-reflecting film, or a special prism. These divert a small amount of light away from the main beam to the guiding eyepiece.

Films and exposures

The selection of the film to be used for a particular object is largely a matter for experiment, as much depends upon the equipment and the photographer. There also has to be a compromise between the acceptable grain size, the

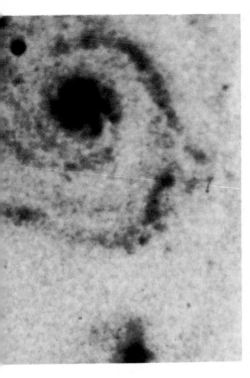

Negative photographs, such as the one on the left, may sometimes show more details than normal prints. This is M51, a spiral galaxy in Canes Venatici.

length of exposure which can be given, and the degree of enlargement. Very fast films may allow short exposures and take advantage of short periods of good seeing, but their grain may not allow much enlargement in the darkroom, if the final picture is to remain acceptable.

When plenty of light is available, such as with the Moon, a slow-speed black-and-white film will give fine-grained negatives which can be greatly enlarged. With fainter objects, such as planets, faster films can be chosen, but many experienced photographers are prepared to retain slower-speed films for the sake of the reduced grain-size, at the expense of longer exposures, and more arduous guiding. Colour films, because of their structure, are less suitable for big enlargements, and may also show colour shifts in long exposures. With some films the sky background may become green, as they record the faint airglow emission. Others, less sensitive in that particular range, retain a black background. (However, many colour casts can be removed either by exposing through a suitable filter – usually for a longer period of time – or by subsequent work in the darkroom.)

The eye is relatively insensitive to colours at low light levels (page 170), so photographs usually show stronger hues. Black-and-white films are insensitive to red light, and very sensitive to blue, so that many stars have photographic magnitudes which differ from the visual ones. A light yellow filter (such as a Wratten 8) will produce an approximately visual response, but requires longer exposures to reach the same limiting magnitude.

The shift in response with colour films is actually an example of reciprocity failure, often mentioned as a problem with astronomical photography. Film speeds are normally calculated on the basis of exposures of a few seconds at the very most. An astronomical exposure, perhaps hundreds of times as long, will not produce a corresponding increase in the darkening of the emulsion. However, all this really means is that exposures must be established on a trial-and-error basis, rather than by following the usual relationship. With all long-exposure photography it is essential to record the exact times of the beginning and end of each exposure, as well as full details of the equipment used.

Colour transparency films are particularly suitable for wide-field photographs of constellations, and the Milky Way. Aurorae and noctilucent clouds are also very realistically rendered. The very fast films now available, although rather grainy, do allow very short exposures, and may be 'push-processed' to give even higher speeds. Colour negative (print) films are not so popular, even though some very fast films are now available, but black-and-white material is extensively used for all forms of astronomical photography. The newer chromogenic films with their extended range of permissible exposures have proved to be very satisfactory for some subjects, such as star fields, with objects differing greatly in brightness.

It is an advantage if you can process astronomical films at home, as this allows individual processing techniques to be developed. Astronomical subjects are not handled particularly well by most commercial organizations, for obvious reasons, so you will have greater control if you are able to do your own processing. If you do have films commercially developed, make sure that you request them to be returned uncut, as astronomical images may confuse both automatic slide-mounting machines and human handlers. In any case it is often necessary to see the edge of the frame to make certain positional measurements.

Left: *A 25-second, fixed-camera exposure of Orion (ASA 200 film, 50 mm f/2.8 lens) reaches about the naked-eye limit.*

Below: *A 5-minute, driven exposure with a 135 mm lens shows fainter stars in the top of Orion*

Over page: *A rayed aurorial band in front of the stars of Hercules, Corona Borealis and Boötes. Photograph by Harry Ford, Dundee, 1981, October 20/21.*

Exploring the sky

Zodiacal light and the gegenschein

If the atmosphere is clear before dawn or after sunset, and when there is no interference from moonlight, you may be able to see the zodiacal light: a pale, tapering glow extending up into the sky. When conditions are good, it is visible in the west after sunset, and in the east before sunrise, when its light has frequently been mistaken for the true dawn. As it actually forms an elliptical area centred on the Sun, and with its longest dimension almost exactly along the ecliptic, it is best observed when the ecliptic is highest in the sky. For northern observers this occurs in the west in spring, and in the east in autumn. In the southern hemisphere the seasons are correspondingly reversed. Observers in the equatorial region are particularly well-placed and it can usually be seen at all seasons.

The zodiacal light is caused by scattering of sunlight by tiny interplanetary particles, mainly those between the orbit of the Earth and the Sun. Other particles do exist outside the Earth's orbit, but these only weakly scatter light back towards the Sun and the Earth. (They are thought to be so dark that they are unlikely to reflect much light at all.) However, at a point on the ecliptic exactly opposite to that of the Sun, you may be lucky enough to see a weak, elliptical glow known as the gegenschein. Extremely faint bridges of light also exist joining the main areas of zodiacal light and the gegenschein, but these are

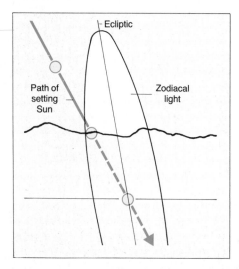

The thin, tapering cone of the zodiacal light is best seen when the ecliptic is high above the horizon.

not readily detectable without specialized equipment, although they have been glimpsed by some keen-eyed observers.

The main region of the zodiacal light has been compared at its brightest to that of the central regions of the Milky Way. Try photographing it with a driven or undriven camera, giving an exposure (on medium-speed film) of 10 to 30 minutes. Such a photograph will probably show a far greater extent than was visible to the naked eye, usually being noticeably wider. However, for best results you will have to use a wide-angle lens, certainly less than 24 mm (with 35 mm cameras), if at all possible. Take care that the sky background or the morning twilight does not build up and reduce the contrast. The gegenschein has been photographed, with some difficulty, but requires exposures of at least 30 minutes. You will certainly need a fast, wide-angle lens to capture this very faint, low-contrast feature in a satisfactory manner.

It is possible to confuse the zodiacal light with certain atmospheric effects – apart from artificial lights – most especially the occasional bright glows caused when volcanic activity has injected material into the upper atmosphere. In general though, these, like the normal twilight arch, are part of a circular area centred on the Sun, as distinct from the tapering zodiacal light.

The cone of the zodiacal light photographed over the eastern horizon and in front of the constellation of Leo. The planets Saturn, Jupiter and Mars are also shown.

Aurorae

The Aurorae Borealis (the name means 'Northern Dawn') and the Aurora Australis, its southern counterpart, occur most frequently in two irregular zones surrounding the Earth's magnetic poles, and lying roughly between latitudes 60° and 70°. However, aurorae have been seen at Singapore close to the magnetic equator, so wherever you are on Earth you may hope to see a display, even if only at rare intervals. Undoubtedly many events go unrecorded because observers have not realized what they were seeing.

Aurorae are formed when electrically-charged particles cascade down from the Earth's magnetosphere – its magnetic sphere of influence – into the upper atmosphere. There the highly energetic particles excite various atoms and cause them to emit visible light. The greatest number of aurorae occur at heights of 100-115 km (about 60-70 miles) but they have been observed quite frequently as low as 70 km (43 miles) and as high as 300 km (around 185 miles). On very rare occasions they have been known to extend to 1000 km (about 620 miles). These altitudes can be compared with the approximately 80 km (50 miles) of noctilucent clouds (page 112) and the 150-50 km (95-30 miles) of most meteors (page 113).

The amount of auroral activity is fairly closely linked with the sunspot cycle (page 142), but generally peaks about one or two years after sunspot maximum. Individual energetic solar flares frequently produce strong auroral displays, and a recurrence 26-28 days later is often noted, after one solar rotation, due to the persistence of particular active regions on the surface.

Aurorae can occur in a number of different forms and these may be further subdivided on the basis of their structure and activity. Frequently observers only see the top of displays appearing over the horizon towards the pole, and this may make identification difficult. Auroral patches may be mistaken for isolated clouds, and the veils or the tops of arcs thought to be areas of fog.

However, in general aurorae do not obscure the stars to quite such an extent as clouds or fog.

Try to obtain measurements of the extent of aurorae and how these change with time. These are quite simple to make, either estimate them by eye or measure them with the simple devices described in many books. The altitude (and azimuth) of the bottom of arcs and bands is the most important piece of information, as with one observation from another site the position and height of the display may be obtained.

The coloration of aurorae can vary greatly, and also depends to a considerable degree upon the observer's eyesight. Pale green and red are most often reported, but other observers of the same display may find it essentially colourless. There is also a variation in colour with height, especially in long-rayed structures. Colour photography with fast films is likely to be of great value in providing information about the distribution in various parts of the displays.

Left: *A well-defined homogeneous arc, showing the distinct lower edge and more diffuse upper border.*

Far left: *Multiple auroral bands, showing the typical 'curtain-like' features as well as distinct rayed structure.*

Photography

Photography of aurorae is very rewarding. Undriven cameras are best for this work, and indeed for serious parallactic work – that is for the determination of positions and heights – the camera should be provided with a rigid mounting allowing it to be pointed at a fixed altitude and azimuth on each occasion. This procedure greatly simplifies the process of calculation. The direction should be agreed with other observers so that the same region of the sky is covered. For a similar reason, although intermediate exposures may be made, try to take photographs beginning at exactly 0, 15, 30 and 45 minutes past each hour (UT). This allows direct comparisons to be made with those of other observers following the same pattern.

Standard and wide-angle lenses are very suitable as these usually have wide apertures and allow short exposures. With apertures of f/1·8 (or similar), exposures of 15-30 seconds on 400 ASA film (colour or black-and-white) may be recommended as a starting point. If the display is very active with considerable motion of the features, you may need shorter exposures to obtain satisfactory, sharp images. Try to ensure that part of the horizon is included in any pictures as this helps to determine the exact altitude of the auroral features from your particular observing site. As with any other astronomical photographs, always record full details of equipment and all times and durations of exposure.

Noctilucent clouds

Noctilucent clouds are high-altitude, atmospheric phenomena occurring at about 80 km (50 miles) and are only observable between latitudes 45° and 60° approximately. They appear (quite frequently) during the weeks around the summer solstice, when twilight persists throughout the 'night', and the Sun is below the horizon for the observer but can still illuminate the clouds. This explains why they cannot be seen closer to the equator. They take the form of very delicate veils, wisps, and wave-like patterns, with a silvery or bluish light, and are sometimes slightly golden towards the horizon. The display may shift its position in the sky, with the ripples and other structures moving in a different, or even opposite, direction. Although they might seem to bear some similarities to ordinary cirrus clouds, they are about 10 times as high, and are betrayed by their appearing around midnight, and their direction (towards the poles). Like aurorae they are usually so thin that they do not obscure the brighter stars.

The exact nature of these clouds remains obscure. They appear to consist of tiny particles coated with ice and which reflect the sunlight. It is uncertain whether the particles are meteoric dust, ions, or even volcanic material injected to particularly high altitudes by violent eruptions (although it appears to be difficult for the latter to take place). Their movements are related to upper-atmosphere winds, but the positions at which they occur and some of their features may possibly be affected by airflow over mountains far below.

A very typical display of noctilucent clouds, photographed (from Scotland) at local midnight.

Noctilucent clouds are interesting in that they appear during the period when auroral observation is most difficult. However, they may be studied with almost identical methods, both visually, when they are classified into a number of different types and also photographically. Make observations at suitable intervals – say every 15 minutes – recording the changes in appearance and general motion of the clouds that take place. Measurements of the angles to various parts of the display are easy to make.

Photography

Photographic techniques are similar to those for auroral observations – ideally with fixed cameras covering the same region of sky as other observers, and making a series of exposures at fixed intervals. As these clouds are brighter than most aurorae you can use either slower films with the advantage of fine grain or else choose smaller apertures. Exposures may have to be reduced, not

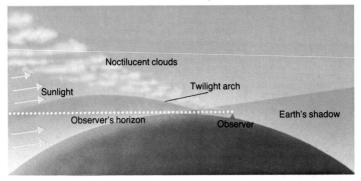

It is only during the summer months that noctilucent clouds can be illuminated by the Sun whilst the observer is in shadow.

because of rapid motion, but because otherwise the bright sky background might fog the film. Colour photography is particularly effective, some films such as Kodachrome giving excellent rendering very similar to the visual appearance. With f/2 lenses and 100 ASA film, you might like to begin by making exposures of 5, 3 and 1 seconds. As with aurorae, aim to start a series of exposures at the exact quarter-hours.

Meteors

When particles or small bodies orbiting the Sun plunge at high speeds into the Earth's atmosphere, ionizing the atoms, they give rise to the streaks of light known as meteors ('shooting stars'). Occasionally these may be very brilliant, if the particles are particularly large. When they are brighter than about magnitude −5, somewhat more than the maximum that Venus can reach, they are called fireballs. The **meteoroids** (as the particles are termed) may be completely burnt up by friction, or else may disintegrate during their passage through the atmosphere. However, if they were sufficiently large when they entered the atmosphere, fragments may survive to fall onto the surface of the Earth, when they are known as **meteorites**. In general any meteorite will have produced a brilliant fireball during its descent.

The recovery of these objects is obviously very important. As yet they are the only celestial bodies that we can examine, apart from the samples returned from the Moon. Even if you are not particularly interested in the fainter meteors, you should at least know what information to record if you observe a fireball.

Observing meteors

You can certainly see meteors on any clear night, and if conditions are good and you are observing with the naked eye, expect there to be 5–10 in an hour. These are **sporadic meteors**, individual particles orbiting alone, and which can appear quite unexpectedly anywhere in the sky. However, at certain times of the year meteors are far more frequent, when an individual **meteor shower** is active. Such showers are caused by groups of particles travelling together along an orbit which, at some point, intersects that of the Earth. It is only while the Earth is close to that particular portion of its own orbit that the members of the shower are seen. Many showers can be linked with known or extinct comets, and it is believed that most of the sporadic meteors have the same general source of origin.

Although shower meteoroids follow parallel paths in space and in the upper atmosphere, perspective makes their tracks appear to diverge from a single

Meteor showers

Shower	Maximum	Normal Limits	Rate at Maxi- mum	Radiant	
				RA	Dec.
				h m	°
Quadrantids	Jan 4	Jan 1-6	70	15 28	+50
Lyrids	Apr 22	Apr 19-25	15	18 08	+32
η Aquarids	May 5	Apr 24-May 20	40	22 20	−01
α Scorpids	Apr 28	Apr 20-May 19	20	16 32	−24
	May 12			16 04	−24
δ Aquarids	Jly 28	Jly 15-Aug 20	20	22 36	−17
				22 04	+02
Perseids	Aug 12	Jly 23-Aug 20	75	03 04	+58
Orionids	Oct 21	Oct 16-26	20	06 24	+15
Taurids	Nov 3	Oct 20-Nov 30	12	03 44	+14
Leonids	Nov 17	Nov 15-20	10	10 08	+22
Puppids-Velids	Dec 8	Nov 27-Jan 9	15	09 00	−48
	Dec 25			09 20	−45
Geminids	Dec 13	Dec 7-15	60	07 28	+32

area of sky, known as the **radiant**. Showers are generally named after the constellations where their radiants are found, and some of the most important are listed in the table. However a few meteor showers have been named after associated comets, and the most important of these which you might come across are probably the Bielids (or Andromedids) and the Giacobinids (or Draconids).

Meteor numbers are always calculated as hourly rates. Those given in the table are only approximate figures and might apply if you were an experienced observer, watching the region of the zenith under very good conditions. Obviously meteors closer to the horizon are dimmed by atmospheric extinction (page 17) and general seeing (page 16) also plays a part. Moonlight causes grave interference for five or six days before and after Full Moon, so in some years, individual showers may be well-nigh impossible to observe. In addition the numbers vary from year to year, either gradually, or dramatically, depending upon whether the particles are spread more or less evenly around the orbit, or are concentrated into dense clumps. The Leonid shower is the most striking example, with high rates in 1799, 1833, and 1866 (and probably earlier in history), but disappointing numbers in 1899 and 1932 when the gravitational effects of Jupiter and Saturn moved the orbit away from the Earth. In 1966, however, there was an astounding display, when the

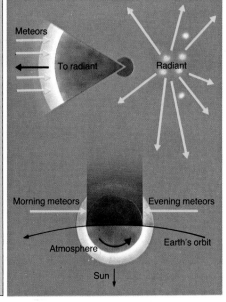

Meteors enter the atmosphere on parallel paths but perspective causes them to appear to diverge from the radiant. Because of the Earth's rotation and orbital motion, more meteors are seen after midnight, when they have higher velocities.

hourly rate rose to about 150000 for a period of around 20 minutes. But it must be added hastily that this number is quite exceptional and that only three of the normal showers (the Quadrantids, Perseids and Geminids) can be expected to exceed rates of 50 per hour.

The number of meteors also changes during the night. Before midnight the only meteors seen are those which are overtaking the Earth, and have slow apparent velocities. After midnight the velocities of the Earth and meteors combine. As the velocity strongly affects the brilliance, the number observed increases after midnight.

Left: *This photograph shows just a few of the thousands of meteors observed during the great Leonid shower of 1966.*

Below: *The Perseid shower has many bright meteors, and a few fireballs.*

Visual observations

The best method of observing meteors visually is for a number of observers to form a group and watch together. Each observer can then cover part of the sky, and one member of the team may act as recorder for the others. However, it is still well worth trying even if you have to observe on your own. Because meteors appear at random intervals you need to be prepared to watch continuously for 30 minutes at a time. (Watches should always last for multiples of 30 minutes, but it is usually just as well to have a break in between.) Make sure that you have enough clothing, as you soon become chilled when sitting (or lying) still for that length of time. Keep a note of the times at which your watches begin and end.

Where should you look? About 45° from the radiant is best, and as always, as high in the sky as possible. One observer cannot hope to cover much of the sky, so do not worry about what might be happening behind you. Obtain a set of charts which you can mount on card and cover with transparent plastic film. (You will usually only need the one showing the part of the sky which you are watching.) If you can, roughly estimate the magnitude of the faintest star which you can see at the beginning and end of each watch. This gives information about the sky conditions so that your observed rates can be corrected as necessary.

Ideally the following details would be recorded for each meteor: time, path, type, brightness, and any special features. If you are observing when a shower is very active it may not be possible to do this for every meteor. The last three pieces of information are then the most important. Let's take the details in order, omitting time, which rarely presents any problems.

PATH   Recording the path is not too difficult. When you see a meteor hold a piece of string, or even better, a straight stick along the path to help to fix its position against the stars. Estimate the start and end points (and another in between if possible). You might say 'a third of the way from γ to α Leonis, over ι Leo, and halfway between δ and γ Vir', for example. Plot the track on the chart. A word of warning here. Meteor paths can be shown as straight lines only on charts with a special form of projection. Such charts are not easy to obtain and are difficult to use as they do not look much like the sky. Meteor tracks on other projections are curved lines, but if you can plot the two end points accurately, any information about the track and orbit can be calculated if necessary. During a shower just note the constellation in which the meteor was seen.

TYPE OF METEOR   Next decide if the meteor belonged to a shower or was sporadic. This can be done by either 'sliding' the stick back along the trail, or mentally projecting the line, to see if it comes from the radiant of any shower active that night. If the line passes within 4° of the position of a radiant, you can safely assume that the meteor belonged to that shower. Draw the position of the radiant on your chart. (A radiant slowly moves as the Earth passes through the meteor stream. Information about the daily motion can be found in one of the astronomical handbooks.)

BRIGHTNESS   Estimates of brightness give a lot of information about the size and velocity of the particles. Unlike variable star methods (page 175) an accuracy of about half a magnitude is all you can hope to obtain. This is not too difficult as you can usually compare a magnitude to that of a star in the area, or say it was halfway between one and another. Don't try to remember lots of magnitudes, just note down the names of the stars (or mark them on the chart), and look up the values afterwards. Try to choose stars close to the meteor's track, so that the extinction (page 17) is about the same. Very bright meteors can be a problem as there may be no suitable comparisons, and you will just have to rely upon your memory of stars such as Sirius (magnitude −1·4), or how bright Jupiter and Venus may become (magnitudes −2·4 and −4·3 respectively).

SPECIAL FEATURES   Some meteors give rise to persistent luminous **trains**, lasting for several seconds or even longer. Make a note of their duration, changes of shape and position. They are not common so any observations are valuable. Other special information may include notable colour and terminal bursts. These features are usually only seen with the brighter meteors.

Photographic observations

Meteor photography is not difficult, but does require patience, as only the brighter meteors are recorded, and many exposures may have to be made before one is captured. Modern fast films and wide-aperture lenses help greatly in this respect. Cameras should be undriven as background star trails will not matter, as long as they can be identified. Like visual work, the best

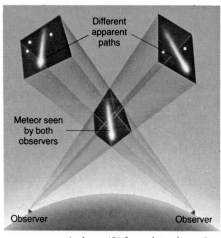

Different apparent paths

Meteor seen by both observers

Observer   Observer

Observation (or photography) of meteors from two different sites allows their heights and paths to be determined.

area to survey is about 45° from the radiant. Some dedicated observers arrange several cameras so that they cover the whole of the sky, others invest in fish-eye lenses. It is quite a good idea to observe the same area by both visual and photographic methods, as then the times of any bright meteors recorded by the camera will be accurately known. Photographs allow information about magnitudes and positions to be obtained with reasonable ease, and have the advantage of providing a permanent record.

If two cameras many kilometres apart are arranged so that their fields cover the same volume of the upper atmosphere, meteor triangulation becomes possible and the exact track of the meteor and its heights can be determined. (Visual observers sometimes co-operate to get similar results.) If possible, the meteors are photographed through a rotating-sector shutter (looking like the blades of a fan) operating in front of the camera lens. This breaks the trail into segments (perhaps 10 a second), from which the actual velocity of the meteor can be derived. In this way it may even be possible to find the precise orbit which it had in space. Changes in the spacing of the segments of the trail show how the body was braked by the upper atmosphere, and can lead to a determination of its density.

Telescopic work

Deliberate meteor watches with binoculars or telescopes are only really suitable for very dedicated observers. The fields of view are restricted, but fainter meteors become visible, giving information about the smaller sizes of meteoroids. However, if you are observing something else – variable stars, galaxies, etc. – you may well see the occasional meteor. Try to record the necessary information about direction, magnitude, colour and speed, or better still make a quick sketch of the field and track. Any observations are valuable as many are needed before proper analysis becomes possible.

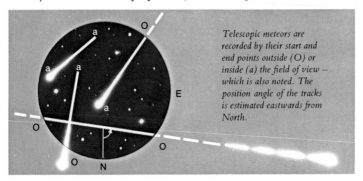

Telescopic meteors are recorded by their start and end points outside (O) or inside (a) the field of view – which is also noted. The position angle of the tracks is estimated eastwards from North.

Fireballs

Any meteor brighter than magnitude −5 is known as a fireball. Some fireballs may be exceptionally brilliant, ranging beyond magnitude −15. (The Full Moon is magnitude −13.) If they are seen at night all the usual techniques apply, but duplicate photographs are particularly valuable as they help to determine whether any meteorite may have fallen to Earth, and where this is likely to be.

Very occasionally fireballs are so brilliant that they can be seen in daylight. Any observations are then of outstanding importance. If you should be lucky enough to see one make a note of the time, make a guess at its brightness, and establish its path. You will not have stars to act as reference points, but you can

A very bright fireball photographed by a stationary all-sky camera (with fish-eye lens).

estimate the altitude and azimuth of the beginning and end of the path, or refer to landmarks on the ground. If you can, establish your exact position and make a note of that. Then wait. The largest fireballs can cause sonic booms and these may take several minutes to reach you. If you note the times at which you hear them the distance to the track can be established. Report any details to your national fireball organization immediately, who may well send an investigator to check some of the details with you, especially if a meteorite fall might be involved. Fireballs may sometimes be confused with satellite re-entries, but there are ways in which they may be distinguished from one another.

Artificial satellites

There are so many objects in orbit around the Earth that observing sessions in the early evening or before dawn rarely pass without some satellites being visible as they pass across the sky. ('Satellites' can, of course, be taken to include spent upper stage rockets, shrouds, and miscellaneous bits and pieces as well as the active satellites themselves.) Many of these objects are rotating or tumbling in their orbits, and show distinct flashes or changes in brightness as sunlight is reflected from large flat surfaces (such as solar panels) and other parts of the structure. They may also disappear or reappear as their paths take them through the Earth's shadow.

It is only when the observer is in shadow and the satellite in sunlight that any object can be seen. As a result the periods of visibility vary with the observer's latitude and the time of year, and also depend on the satellite's orbital height and inclination. In summer a high-orbit satellite may be visible at any time during the night for an observer at high latitudes. At other times the same satellite may be visible for only a very short period low on the horizon. This means that prediction of the times when individual satellites are visible from

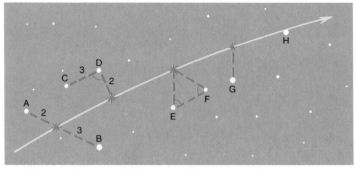

A satellite's position is given by the ratio when it crosses a line between two stars (A & B) or is at right angles to a pair (C & D). Other positions are when it forms an equilateral triangle with two stars (E & F), is vertically above a star (G) or passes close to another (H).

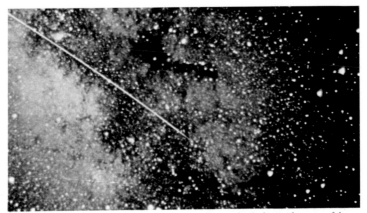

An early, and very bright satellite, Echo II, crossing the star clouds close to the centre of the Galaxy.

any place is fairly complicated. It can be carried out by those who like such calculations, but most observers rely upon precise predictions issued by national co-ordinating bodies. (Approximate times of appearance for a few bright objects are given in some newspapers.) Once an expected track has been plotted on a chart, observations can be made with binoculars or larger telescopes, the former being most suitable for the majority of amateurs.

Serious observing involves defining the position of a satellite at a particular time, determined by a stopwatch or other means. The most accurate method is to note when the satellite passes between two stars, but this is not always possible, and other determinations sometimes have to be used. At least two positions are needed on each pass for the orbit to be determined. Comparison of the predicted and observed paths then allows deductions to be made about the density of the upper atmosphere (particularly where the satellite is closest to the Earth, at perigee) which fluctuates with solar activity, and also about the exact size and shape of the Earth. Observations of the magnitude and flash rate gives information about the condition of the satellite itself.

Satellites move so slowly that they are rarely taken for other objects, but re-entries can be confused with meteors or even bright fireballs. You can usually tell the difference by noting their apparent velocities and directions. Satellites orbit and re-enter slowly at speeds of 4–8 km (2·5–5 miles) per second, whereas the theoretical absolute minimum for a meteoroid is about 11 km (7 miles) per second, and most have speeds far higher than this – up to about 70 km (43 miles) per second. Observing meteors will give you an idea of what apparent speed can be expected.

The direction in which an object is travelling can also provide a useful clue. No artificial satellites travel from east to west, but rather in the opposite direction. Polar-orbiting satellites cross from north to south or from south to north. In addition, satellites frequently break into fragments as they re-enter and produce multiple trails. This is fairly uncommon among natural meteoroids, although it tends to occur with some of the larger fireballs.

The Moon

The Moon is usually the first object that people examine when they start to become interested in astronomy. It seems the obvious choice. It is large (about 30′ in diameter), bright, and easily found. Its brightness, too, means that it is quite possible to observe the Moon in daylight. This is a good idea as it reduces the amount of glare from the surface, and is quite satisfactory provided that the seeing conditions are reasonably steady. If a telescope is used at night, it may be necessary to use a neutral-density filter or else reduce the telescope's aperture to provide more comfortable observing conditions.

Phases of the Moon

The motion of the Moon is extremely complex and the calculation of the exact times of Moonrise and Moonset is very complicated. You will probably find that the details given in many newspapers are quite adequate, but if you need very accurate information you will have to use one of the astronomical yearbooks. On average the Moon rises and sets each day about 50 minutes later than the day before, but the amount varies very greatly.

A complete cycle of the familiar lunar phases from one New Moon to the next takes approximately 29·5 days, or one **lunation**. The Moon's age is reckoned from the time of New Moon, when it is, of course, closest to the Sun, or may even pass in front of its disk in a solar eclipse (page 142). Many people enjoy the challenge of trying to spot the hair-thin crescent when it is merely a few hours old, and the technique suggested for locating Mercury may prove useful (page 151).

Below (left to right): *The Moon aged 4, 10, 14 (Full), 17·8 and 26 days. The rays become visible at Full Moon.*

Above: *An Apollo II photograph (north at top), showing part of both near and far sides, with Mare Crisium near the centre of the disk.*

Key to Moon Map

The two approximate ages of the Moon when a feature is best seen are indicated by the figures following the name. These dates may vary by a day, owing to libration and other factors.

1 Taruntius	4:18	51 Mercator	10:24
2 Proclus	14:18	52 Schickard	12:26
3 Macrobius	4:18	53 Delambre	6:20
4 Cleomedes	3:17	54 Hipparchus	7:21
5 Geminus	3:17	55 Albategnius	7:21
6 Franklin	4:18	56 Ptolomaeus	8:22
7 Posidonius	5:19	57 Alphonsus	8:22
8 Atlas	4:18	58 Arzachel	8:22
9 Hercules	5:19	59 Thebit	8:22
10 Endymion	3:17	60 Birt	8:22
11 Bürg	5:19	61 Purbach	8:22
12 Eudoxus	6:20	62 Werner	7:21
13 Aristoteles	6:20	63 Aliacencis	7:21
14 Plinius	6:20	64 Walter	7:21
15 Agrippa	7:21	65 Deslandres	8:22
16 Rima Ariadaeus	6:20	66 Pitatus	8:22
17 Julius Caesar	6:20	67 Orontius	8:22
18 Manilius	7:21	68 Saussure	8:22
19 Cassini	7:21	69 Tycho	8:22
20 Mons Piton	8:22	70 Wilhelm	9:23
21 Vallis Alpes	8:22	71 Longomontanus	9:23
22 Mons Pico	8:22	72 Maginus	8:22
23 Plato	8:22	73 Clavius	9:23
24 Meton	6:20	74 Blancanus	9:23
25 Barrow	7:21	75 Scheiner	10:24
26 Anaxagoras	9:23	76 Stöfler	7:21
27 Philolaus	9:23	77 Maurolycus	6:20
28 Anaximenes	11:25	78 Vlacq	5:19
29 Pythagoras	12:26	79 Hommel	5:19
30 Aristillus	7:21	80 Pitiscus	5:19
31 Autolycus	7:21	81 Rabbi Levi	6:20
32 Archimedes	8:22	82 Zagut	6:20
33 Timocharis	8:22	83 Janssen	4:18
34 Aristarchus	11:25	84 Metius	4:18
35 Herodotus	11:25	85 Piccolomini	5:19
36 Va. Schröteri	11:25	86 Fracastorius	5:19
37 Mons Rümker	12:26	87 Abulfeda	6:20
38 Pallas	8:22	88 Catharina	6:20
39 Eratosthenes	8:22	89 Cyrillus	6:20
40 Copernicus	9:23	90 Theophilus	5:19
41 Reinhold	9:23	91 Mädler	5:19
42 Landsberg	10:24	92 Gutenberg	5:19
43 Kepler	10:24	93 Goclenius	4:18
44 Fra Mauro	9:23	94 Langrenus	3:17
45 Grimaldi	13-14:27-28	95 Petavius	3:17
46 Letronne	11:25	96 Snellius	3:17
47 Billy	12:26		
48 Gassendi	11:25		
49 Bullialdus	9:23		
50 Campanus	10:24		

As the Sun's elevation changes throughout the seasons, so too does that of the Moon. As a result the best time for studying a particular phase falls at a specific time of year. The Full Moon is best examined in midwinter, when the Sun is lowest and the Moon highest. The crescent phases around New Moon, on the other hand, may well be better at midsummer. For studying First Quarter northern-hemisphere observers should choose the spring (autumn for those in the south). Similarly Last Quarter is best in autumn for northern astronomers and in spring for southern observers. The Moon's motion 5° on either side of the ecliptic has an additional effect upon visibility at these particular times. Observers in the tropics are lucky in that they are able to observe at any time of the year, but then the periods of visibility are not so long.

Lunar features

Some lunar features can be seen even by the naked eye and, as already mentioned (page 26), you will find that it really is worthwhile trying to make a drawing of these without any optical aid, particularly as training for planetary observation. The dark areas may be easily outlined, but sharp-eyed

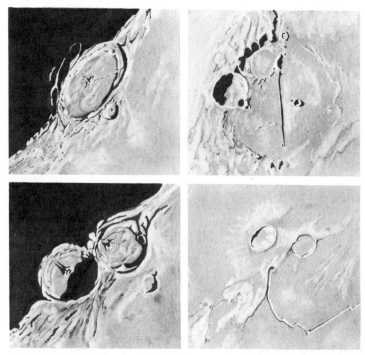

Four drawings by J. D. Greenwood. Top left: *Petavius.* Top right: *Mare Nubium, the crater Birt and Rupes Recta.* Above left: *Cyrillus and Theophilus.* Above right: *Aristarchus, Herodotus and Vallis Schröteri.*

observers can also make out some of the details in the brighter portions, especially when the changing shadows throw some parts into relief.

Binoculars begin to show that the dark and light areas are very different. The bright regions prove to be rugged, cratered highlands (occasionally known as the *terrae*), quite distinct from the lower, smoother, dark plains. The Latin term *mare*, or 'sea' (plural *maria*) is still retained for most of these low-lying areas as a reminder of the days when they were wrongly thought to be bodies of water. The largest of the craters are shown fairly distinctly with binoculars, but even the smallest telescopes reveal a far greater wealth of detail. Craters of all shapes and sizes are visible with a 75-mm telescope as well as many other features such as the valley-like rilles, ridges, isolated peaks, and extensive mountain ranges. Like many other astronomical objects, lunar features have internationally-known, official, Latin names, and these are used here. The general terms for the various types of feature are listed in the table.

The continual variation in the elevation of the Sun means that the appearance of the features and their shadows are also changing all the time. Many of the details are seen most clearly when they are close to the **terminator** (the line dividing the illuminated and non-illuminated portions of the surface). It is then, at sunrise and sunset, that the low angle of the lighting causes everything to appear in exaggerated relief. In fact, the Moon's rugged appearance is mostly an illusion caused by the dramatic, high-contrast lighting. Most of the slopes on the Moon are very gentle and are much less than those found on the Earth.

Under high illumination some features, even very large craters, become indistinct or virtually disappear, or may only be seen by virtue of the different amount of light which they reflect when compared with the surrounding surface. A few features may become more conspicuous because of this effect. The most notable examples are the ray systems extending from some of the craters. These are hardly visible at early and late phases, but are most conspicuous under a high Sun, around the time of Full Moon.

The Earth itself, being covered with clouds and areas of ice, reflects a considerable amount of sunlight back into space. It is said to have a high

Lunar Features

Term	Feature	Example
Mare (Maria)	'Sea' – Flat lava plain(s)	Mare Humorum
Mons	Mountain	Mons Pico
Montes	Mountain range	Montes Altai
Palus	'Swamp' – Irregular dark plain	Palus Putredinis
Rima(e)	Rille(s) or cleft(s)	Rima Ariadaeus
Rupes	Fault	Rupes Recta
Sinus	'Bay' – Mare area	Sinus Iridum
Vallis	Valley	Vallis Alpes

albedo. When the Moon is a thin crescent, a few days before or after New Moon, this reflected 'Earthshine' can be seen illuminating the portion of the surface otherwise in shadow. Some of the lunar features (especially craters such as Aristarchus, Kepler and Copernicus) themselves have high albedos, and can be distinctly seen by this dim reflected light.

Libration

The Moon always turns the same face to the Earth, and at first this may seem to be unvarying. Closer attention over a period of a few lunations shows that alterations in the visibility of the features do take place. These are the result of the effects known as libration, which make the Moon appear to rock slowly backwards and forwards before our eyes.

The inclination of the Moon's orbit takes it above and below the plane of the Earth's equator, causing libration in latitude so that we alternately see more of the northern hemisphere and then more of the southern. Due to the Moon's elliptical orbit around the Earth its speed varies quite considerably. However, it rotates on its axis at a constant rate, and as the two cannot match all round the orbit, libration in longitude results. Parts of the farside appear and disappear over the eastern and western limbs. (The **limb** is the apparent edge of any body which shows a distinct disk.)

Various other libration effects also combine with those mentioned to expose about 59% of the surface to view over a very long (30-year) period. Some of the formations on the edge of this visible region are very rarely seen under favourable lighting conditions. Due to libration, the terminator does not sweep across the various formations with monotonous regularity every month, but may reach a particular feature as much as half a day earlier or later than average.

There is also a change in the Moon's size between the nearest and farthest points in its orbit (**perigee** and **apogee**) which, although not apparent to the eye, shows on photographs taken at those times and given the same degree of enlargement. However, unlike libration, this has no effect upon observations.

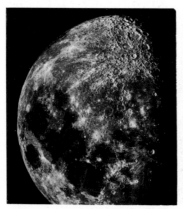

The surface of the Moon

Start to observe the lunar features by following the passage of both the sunrise and sunset terminators across the disk, watching the individual formations appear and disappear in turn. A guide to the position of the terminator and to the visibility of individual formations on any particular day of the lunation is given in the tables on this and succeeding pages.

The features at the limbs are difficult to observe around the time of New Moon, so they must be studied just before and after it is Full. These are, of course, the regions most affected by libration, so individual features given in the list may not always be visible. Due to the effects of foreshortening it is frequently very difficult to interpret the details at the limbs, and positive identification of features may prove to be impossible. Only repeated observation will enable this to be done with any degree of confidence.

Maria

We now know that the dark mare areas of the Moon have been flooded with lava. In some cases (the circular maria) this has filled basins excavated by the impact of large meteoroids. Mare Imbrium is the most notable example, but others are Mare Serenitatis, Mare Humorum and Mare Crisium. Other maria are irregular and less well-defined; Mare Frigoris and Mare Vaporum are good examples. Oceanus Procellarum is so vast, covering over 2 000 000 sq km (800 000 sq miles) that it is really in a class by itself. Several of the maria exhibit extensive wrinkle ridges, the most prominent being those in Mare Serenitatis and Oceanus Procellarum, although there are others in Mare Tranquillitatis. (The last region is probably best known as the site of the first Moon-landing.)

Far left and left: *The effects of libration show in the changing shape of Mare Crisium (left) and by features close to the limb of the Moon.*

Right: *The region of Mare Serenitatis and Posidonius – the latter shown in the series of drawings on pages 94/5.*

Mountain ranges

Some of the Moon's most conspicuous mountain ranges form the edges of maria. The Montes Carpatus, Apenninus and Alpes (with the distinctive Vallis Alpes) around Mare Imbrium, and the Montes Caucasus bordering Mare Serenitatis are very notable. The Rupes Altai is rather different, and appears to be an old formation that has been degraded and partially overlaid by later deposits.

Part of the Mare Imbrium, the Montes Alpes and the dark-floored crater Plato.

Individual isolated peaks are also encountered such as Pico and Piton in Mare Imbrium and the ill-defined mass of Mons Rümker at the junction of Sinus Roris and Oceanus Procellarum. The closest that the Moon comes to distinct volcanic structures are the low domes, such as those near the craters Arago and Hortensius.

Craters

Impacts by meteoroids (page 113) were responsible for the craters which are the most conspicuous characteristic of the Moon. They cover a vast range of sizes. Some of the largest are well-defined, such as Ptolemaeus, Schickard and the enormous but rarely-visible crater, Bailly which is 300 km (185 miles) in diameter. Others, for example Hipparchus and Fra Mauro, are very degraded.

Many craters such as Copernicus and Theophilus have terraces on their interior walls, while central peaks are fairly common as in Petavius, Eratosthenes, Copernicus, Aristillus, and Theophilus. There are an innumerable number of smaller, fairly regular, bowl-shaped craters, down to the limit of visibility. In the lunar highlands craters frequently overlap and break into one another. Thebit has a well-formed small crater (Thebit A) centred on its wall, and is probably the best example.

Some smaller craters are very distinctive, such as those in the crater chain on the floor of Clavius, and the dark-haloed pits in the floor of Alphonsus. Distinct internal details are seen in some craters, perhaps the most famous being the dark bands within Aristarchus.

SECONDARY CRATERS AND RAYS   Secondary craters are formed when material thrown out by the main impact itself excavates smaller craters. Such patterns and blankets of ejecta are distinctly visible, especially around Copernicus and Bullialdus. Other, finer ejecta have produced the pale ray-systems spreading out over the surface, and visible at Full Moon. Tycho's system is the most extensive and the crater itself is a major feature with a central peak and a definite dark halo. Copernicus, Kepler, and Aristarchus also have conspicuous rays, while those of Proclus are very asymmetrical. In Mare Fecunditatis, the pair of craters Messier and Messier A present a comet-like appearance with their one prominent ray. It is thought that they were formed by a low-angle impact which threw most of the material in a single direction.

FLOODED CRATERS   Some craters have very dark floors, indicating flooding by lava. Endymion, Archimedes, Plato and Grimaldi are some of the most notable examples. Some craters have quite obviously been breached by mare lava flows, and in the case of Sinus Iridum this is particularly conspicuous. Prinz, Letronne and Fracastorius are some other features of this type. The interior of Wargentin has been flooded up to the level of the rim, giving rise to a plateau.

Left: *Sinus Iridum is the remnant of a large crater that has been flooded by lava from Mare Imbrium.*

Below: *The crater Tycho has a distinct dark halo and is the source of the largest ray system.*

There are large numbers of ruined formations, but a few are truly called 'ghòst' craters. These are old features apparently completely covered by flows of lava, which on cooling has contracted, producing a mere suggestion of the underlying structure. Stadius in Sinus Aestuum between the craters of Eratosthenes and Copernicus is the best example, but another is south of Lambert in Mare Imbrium, and Lamont in Mare Tranquillitatis is rather more prominent.

Rilles

Other common types of formation are the various kinds of rilles and clefts (which are all given the general Latin term *rima*). Some of these appear to be directly related to the formation of individual features such as the clefts which run parallel to the borders of Mare Humorum. Rilles which may be less obviously structural are prominent in the Triesnecker, Ariadaeus and Hyginus systems, all of which are in the area bounded by Sinus Medii, Mare Vaporum and Mare Tranquilitatis.

The ruined crater Julius Caesar and the Ariadaeus rille system, close to the centre of the Moon's visible disk.

Sinuous rilles are rather different, and owe their winding nature to the fact that they formed from lava tubes, the roofs of which later collapsed. Vallis Schröteri (close to Aristarchus) is possibly the best example, while the similar Prinz rilles are nearby. The great rift of Vallis Alpes has a narrow, sinuous rille on its floor, and Rima Hadley (the site of the Apollo 15 landing) is another good example.

Rifted floors occur in some craters, such as Gassendi, Petavius, and Posidonius, while a rift passes through both walls and floor of Goclenius, continuing the line of a cleft outside the crater. The most distinct single fault is the Rupes Recta (often known as the 'Straight Wall') in Mare Nubium – very striking at sunset, but in reality with quite a gentle slope of only about 7°. Rupes Cauchy is more like a cleft, but casts a conspicuous shadow only at sunrise.

Transient phenomena

There are particular areas of the Moon which occasionally show changes in brightness. These Transient Lunar Phenomena (TLPs) – known in North America as Lunar Transient Phenomena (LTPs) – are of uncertain origin, but may be related to solar activity, or to the occasional escape of gas from the lunar interior. They cause short-lived colour changes to the areas affected, and may be studied by examining the surface through red and blue filters. The simplest device – called a 'Moon-blink' – allows these to be switched rapidly backwards and forwards, when any change in brightness becomes immediately apparent. Some areas, such as Fracastorius, show permanent 'blinks', but others, particularly Aristarchus, Gassendi and Alphonus, are the sites of definite activity.

Lunar eclipses

Eclipses of the Moon occur when it passes through the Earth's shadow. This can only happen at Full Moon, but because of the inclination of the orbit to the ecliptic, on most occasions the Moon does not encounter the shadowed zone. However, two or three eclipses occur every year and each one is visible to any observer on the hemisphere facing the Moon. The motion of the Moon through the shadow is always from west to east.

There are two regions to the Earth's shadow: an inner dark cone pointing away from the Earth (the **umbra**), and wider, less dense cone with its apex at the Sun (the **penumbra**). Although penumbral eclipses occur if the Moon's path crosses just this region, they are of little interest, as the light is only slightly

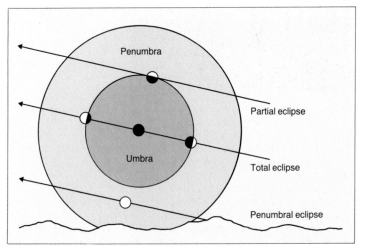

The exact path of the Moon through the Earth's shadow determines the type of lunar eclipse that takes place.

dimmed and the change is rarely noticeable. Partial eclipses result when part of the Moon passes through the umbral cone, but most attention is given to total eclipses when it is fully immersed. The maximum duration of totality (the period when the Moon is fully eclipsed) comes when the Moon crosses the centre of the shadow, and can amount to 1 hour 42 minutes.

As the Earth's atmosphere refracts some light into even the centre of the umbra, the Moon usually remains visible throughout the eclipse. However, blue light is scattered in the lower atmosphere, so red light predominates and the Moon consequently appears that colour. But this is not always the case, and sometimes the Moon has become very dark, or may even have disappeared. The degree of darkness seems to be influenced by several factors, including solar activity, volcanic eruptions and meteor showers. (Volcanic and meteoric particles can persist in the atmosphere for months, causing increased scattering and darker eclipses.) You can estimate the colour and darkness of an eclipse by using the scale developed by Danjon, and you may find that the value changes during the eclipse.

In a total eclipse, apart from the outlines of the maria, some of the craters may remain visible, especially Aristarchus, Copernicus, Kepler and Tycho. This could be due in part to luminescence of some lunar materials, but the cause remains quite uncertain. Note down any of these or other features that you are able to see. You might also like to try to obtain a series of drawings during the course of the eclipse, and this is a good opportunity to make some coloured sketches.

It is interesting to time the various events during an eclipse. The most obvious are the first and second contacts when the Moon just touches and fully enters the umbra, and the corresponding third and fourth contacts on the way out. In the same way note the times when individual craters enter and leave the umbra. Such timings give information about the way in which the Earth's

During a total lunar eclipse the Moon is only seen by red light, refracted into the shadow by the Earth's atmosphere.

atmosphere affects the size of the shadow. A very simple observation is to note the time when it first becomes apparent to the naked eye that an eclipse is happening. This may seem so easy that it can be of little use, but in fact it helps us to judge the accuracy of pre-telescopic observations. They in turn give information about how the Earth's rotation rate has been changing over the centuries.

Danjon lunar eclipse scale

	0	Very dark, Moon nearly invisible at mid-totality.
	1	Dark grey or brownish, few details visible
	2	Dark- or rust-red with darker central area, outer regions quite bright
	3	Brick-red, frequently with a yellowish border
	4	Coppery or orange colour, very bright with sometimes a bluish border

Lunar and other occultations

An **appulse** is an apparently close approach between two celestial bodies. Photographs taken on such occasions can be very striking, as can those when planets are near nebulae and clusters. It is well worth keeping an eye on planetary positions with such possibilities in mind.

When the Moon, planets or minor planets pass between the Earth and another object (usually a star), an **occultation** takes place. Lunar occultations are quite frequent but the motion of the Moon is so complex that many years may elapse before it again occults any particular star. Occultations by other bodies are much rarer, and can usually only be seen from a very restricted area of the Earth, so they are quite a challenge to observers.

For any occultations you need to obtain predictions, and these are published in the yearly handbooks, or are supplied by various national and international organizations. Once again the position of the observer on the Earth makes a lot of difference. Observations provide information about the positions, sizes and shapes of the occulting bodies, and about the positions and nature of the objects occulted. For the best use to be made of the information the latitude, longitude, and height above sea level of the observing site should be known as accurately as possible.

The Moon serves as a useful example. As it moves across the sky stars disappear on the eastern side and reappear in the west as viewed by the observer. Because of the lack of lunar atmosphere these events normally happen instantaneously, and may come as quite a shock, especially when they occur at the dark limb. (When you begin it is a good idea to observe events in the first part of the lunation, as Earthshine enables the dark limb to be seen, and so provides some warning of the disappearance.) Gradual, or stepped events are sometimes caused by close binary systems (page 177). The bright limb naturally causes considerable interference due to glare, so it is usual to

A planetary conjunction. Mercury, Venus, Mars and Jupiter appear with the Moon and several bright stars.

observe disappearances before Full Moon, and reappearances in the later half of the lunation. Bright stars are the exception as both events may be seen. It is of advantage to use a telescope with a high focal ratio, or at least with a high magnification, so that less of the Moon is in the field of view. The intensity of the light is also reduced (page 73), making the star easier to see.

Disappearances present few problems as the stars can be easily located, but reappearances are a little more difficult. An equatorial mount with setting circles is obviously the best solution, but otherwise the predicted position angle (page 178) of reappearance will have to be used. On an equatorial mount a wide-field eyepiece with a crosswire arranged to show the line of drift will enable the point of reappearance to be established, if the point of disappearance has been observed.

Observing occultations may be undertaken with almost any size of instrument. Similarly the equipment required for recording the times of the events need not be very complicated; ordinary analogue or digital stop-watches are frequently used and various other methods exist. The problems arise in knowing the *precise* Universal Time (to an accuracy of a fraction of a second) at which events occur. Obviously you cannot use an ordinary clock or digital watch, however accurate these may seem to be for ordinary purposes or other observational work. Any timing equipment must therefore be calibrated against accurate time signals, and these are usually obtained from telephone or short-wave radio services, the latter having the greatest accuracy. Checks are carried out before and after the events so that any changes in rate of the timing device may be established. Taking all these precautions and observing with care, experienced observers may achieve accuracies of one-tenth of a second. There will be differences between their timings and those of other observers due to the variation in personal reaction times – an effect known as **personal equation** – but these may usually be taken into account in the full analysis of the observations.

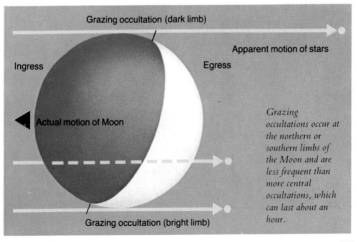

Grazing occultation (dark limb)

Apparent motion of stars

Ingress

Egress

Actual motion of Moon

Grazing occultations occur at the northern or southern limbs of the Moon and are less frequent than more central occultations, which can last about an hour.

Grazing occultation (bright limb)

Grazing occultations

Grazing occultations occur when a star appears to just brush the Moon's northern or southern limb. Irregularities in the surface mean that it may then disappear and reappear several times. These events are fascinating to observe, so try not to miss one that occurs in your area. However, they do require even more preparation than normal occultations. There is only a narrow track on the Earth's surface where any particular graze maybe seen, so it may be necessary to take a portable telescope to a suitable site. Ideally, several observers should position themselves in a line across the track as then an accurate profile of the Moon can be drawn from the various timings.

Timing is much more difficult as the star may not only disappear and reappear several times, but also flash out in a narrow lunar valley. The best method is to record both time signals and event markers on the same tape recorder. The 'marks' can be spoken words ('In' and 'Out', for example), 'clicks' made by any suitable means, or better still, a continuous tone produced while the star is invisible. If simultaneous time signals cannot be received by radio, then one has to be obtained by telephone before the event, and the recorder kept running until a second signal has been received after the graze. This is less accurate as temperature changes and declining battery power may alter the recording rate. But with care, it can still give quite good results.

In this photograph Venus has just reappeared at the dark limb after occultation by the Moon.

Other occultations

The Moon may also occult planets and these events are always worth observing and trying to photograph. Occultations by planets are also interesting, but here of course, there can be gradual fading if an atmosphere is present. Observers of Saturn (page 164) may sometimes see a star being occulted by the rings. Watch such an event very carefully, recording any changes in brightness that are seen, as well as whether the star is always visible. Once again, timings should be made as accurately as possible. Occultations by minor planets and their results are described elsewhere (page 159).

The Sun

Never look at the Sun directly, either with the naked eye, or with any form of equipment. Even the smallest lens concentrates enough light onto the eye to produce lasting damage or complete blindness. This is not surprising when you think how dazzling it is when it happens to shine straight into your face. It may be a little weaker when low on the horizon, but it is always too strong to be observed without special precautions.

The safest, and simplest, method is to project an image. Reflectors are not very suitable for this sort of work, unless they are specially constructed, so use a small refractor. (You can try one side of a pair of binoculars if you have nothing else.) Make sure before you start that any finder (or the second objective of the binoculars) is securely covered by a proper cap. Hold a white card behind the eyepiece, and using the shadow of the telescope as a guide, point it towards the Sun. You can adjust the sharpness of the image by moving the card in and out. Do not point any equipment at the Sun for very long, as the concentrated heat could damage the eyepiece, especially if it contains cemented lenses.

Using a card as a projection screen is not very satisfactory, even if a 'sunshade' is fitted to the telescope. Construct a light-weight box, with just a small opening for the eyepiece mount, and another so that you can see the image. Try to adjust the size, and the eyepiece used, so that the solar image is a standard diameter – preferably the long-established size of 6 inches (152 mm).

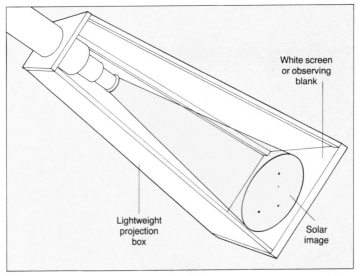

White screen
or observing
blank

Lightweight
projection
box

Solar
image

Projecting an image onto a white screen (in this case in a projection box) is the only safe way of observing the Sun.

Never think of using ordinary filters to observe the Sun directly – none are safe. This includes even the glass, so-called 'Sun' filters occasionally supplied with small refractors. Photographic neutral density and polarizing filters are particularly unsafe, as without your being able to feel anything, they can transmit harmful amounts of infra-red radiation.

Only the specially-made reflecting filters are safe. These, of metal-coated glass or Mylar film, mount in front of the objective, and only allow about 1% or less of the radiation to pass. The whole telescope remains cool, which is highly desirable. Even with the small amount of light that is transmitted, it is still usually necessary to reduce the aperture of the telescope as well.

A proper equatorial mounting is a great convenience. It makes it easier to follow the movement of the Sun, and also helps with orientation. Viewing a projected image may be confusing, but if you move the telescope slightly on each axis in turn, you will soon identify the orientation. With the normal method of projection this is like a naked-eye view but with east and west reversed.

Draw a faint grid of lines on the screen which receives the solar image, and a similar, but heavier grid, exactly the same size, on another piece of card. The second grid will show through a thin drawing blank placed over it, and thus serves to locate the features. When commencing observations, adjust the exact position of the projection box so that either a sunspot or the northern and southern limbs trail along the lines of the grid. (With an altazimuth mount you will have to adjust the orientation at intervals throughout your observing session.)

Solar photography may be carried out quite satisfactorily when a reflecting filter is fitted to the telescope. It is not advisable to try it directly through long-focus lenses without similar precautions, as the heat can easily damage camera shutters.

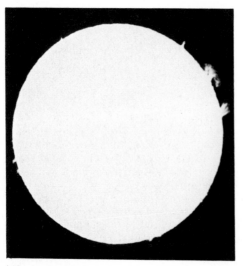

Left: *This amateur photograph was made by special equipment (a spectroheliograph) giving an image in a single wavelength of the spectrum. The long exposure necessary to record the prominences around the limb has overexposed the features on the disk.*

Right: *The major features visible on the Sun are sunspots and faculae, as well as general limb darkening.*

Solar features

The Sun is only a fairly small, average star, 1 392 530 km (about 865 320 miles) in diameter. From the Earth, at a distance of one astronomical unit (147 597 870 km or about 92 960 116 miles), it appears only about 30′ in diameter. It is, nevertheless, the only star that we can yet study in detail, and many features may be observed.

The apparent surface is known as the photosphere. Its most prominent features are **sunspots**. These normally consist of a dark centre (the **umbra**) surrounded by a paler, outer region (the **penumbra**), which under good conditions will often show some radial structure. A few days' observation shows that spots are carried across the disk by the solar rotation. However as the Sun is completely gaseous the rotation period varies between the equator and the poles, and an average apparent period is about 27·27 days. The apparent paths of sunspots around the disk are influenced by the tilt of the solar axis relative to the Earth. At the limb they usually appear considerably foreshortened.

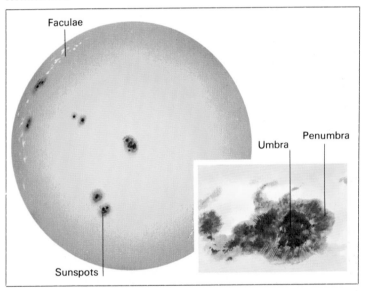

Faculae

Penumbra

Umbra

Sunspots

Sunspots appear dark because they are slightly cooler than the surrounding surface. They are regions where the Sun's magnetic field is particularly strong, and often form in close pairs of opposite magnetic polarity. Complex spot groups also occur and may cover considerable areas of the surface. Individual sunspots may be fairly short-lived, appearing and disappearing in just a few days, but groups and centres of activity may be more persistent, and their evolution can be traced by daily observation during the 7–10 days that they are easily visible on the disk. They may even reappear over the limb after a complete solar rotation. Counting active areas is a relatively simple but very useful observational task.

Overall numbers of spots fluctuate in the 11-year **sunspot cycle**. The cycle actually affects general solar activity, of which sunspots are only a small, easily visible part. The course of an individual cycle begins at minimum when small spots make their appearance at high solar latitudes in each hemisphere, although rarely above 35°. The general centres of activity migrate towards the equator, and at sunspot maximum are concentrated around latitude 15°. After this the number declines, but while the old areas of activity continue to move towards the equator, the first spots of the next cycle begin to form at high latitudes.

Bright patches are known as **faculae**, and exist both before and after sunspots form in the same areas. They are most visible towards the solar limb, unlike the much smaller **granulation** which appears under good conditions on the centre of the disk. This consists of cells with light centres and darker borders, and thus produces a generally mottled appearance. The edges of the Sun always show **limb darkening**, where we are viewing cooler, higher regions than in the centre of the disk.

Solar eclipses

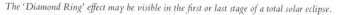

When the Moon passes between the Sun and the Earth at New Moon the three bodies are rarely perfectly aligned, and the Moon's shadow usually misses the Earth. However, at least twice a year, and sometimes as many as five times, the shadow does touch the Earth and produces a solar eclipse.

Like the shadow of the Earth (page 133), the Moon's consists of a dark umbra and a larger penumbra. When just the latter touches the Earth, observers see a partial solar eclipse, only some of the disk being covered. Partial eclipses are not of very great interest to astronomers, although they do give some

The 'Diamond Ring' effect may be visible in the first or last stage of a total solar eclipse.

opportunity for photography. Do please remember that just the same precautions must be followed when observing partial eclipses as with the Sun itself (page 139). *Never look at them directly with the naked eye, through binoculars or a telescope otherwise you will be blinded.*

If the umbra reaches the Earth, a **total eclipse** is produced. Bright stars and planets may become visible in the darkened sky. The zone of totality is only small (no more than about 300 km or 190 miles across at the most), and it is for this reason that total solar eclipses are only rarely seen from any particular place on Earth. The path of totality sweeps across the surface as a result of the combined effects of the Earth's rotation and the motion of the bodies. The maximum duration of the total phase is about 7 minutes 30 seconds, but due to the varying distance of the Moon it can happen that the umbra only 'touches

A partial solar eclipse can only be safely photographed with special filters over the lens of the camera.

down' at one point for a few seconds. In any case, whenever the umbral shadow cone fails to reach the ground, an **annular eclipse** will result. The Sun will not be completely covered but will appear as a ring surrounding the Moon.

Left: *The delicate structure of the solar corona shown at this eclipse is typical of that visible close to sunspot minimum.*

The most conspicuous solar feature revealed at a total eclipse is the **corona**, which spreads far into space. It is the outermost layer of the solar atmosphere, and has a temperature of millions of degrees. Its shape and size change with the sunspot cycle, being more regular at sunspot minimum, but it frequently shows long 'streamers' as well as shorter 'plumes' at the poles. The inner corona may be studied at any time with special equipment, but the outer is seen only at eclipses.

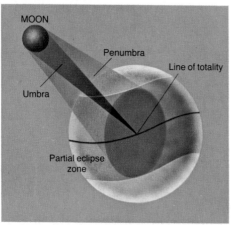

Left: *As the elongated cone of the Moon's shadow sweeps across the Earth, a total eclipse will only be seen in a narrow central track.*

Equally striking are the bright, pinkish **prominences** seen around the limb. These loops and wisps of glowing gas may appear to be material ejected from the surface, but are often gas streaming down from the corona. Some amateurs have special equipment and can see them at other times, even against the solar disk, when they are known as filaments.

When the Moon almost covers the solar disk, brilliant points of light may remain visible through lunar valleys in the effect known as Baily's Beads. At the very beginning and end of totality a single uncovered part of the photosphere may give rise to a striking 'Diamond Ring'.

Observing the planets

If you have a choice, use a refractor, Cassegrain reflector or catadioptric telescope for planetary observations. Their high focal ratios give larger primary images than Newtonian reflectors, and the restricted fields are no disadvantage. If you already have a Newtonian, you can still get excellent results if you use a Barlow lens (page 74) and eyepieces of good quality. A 75-mm refractor is the minimum size for seeing any detail, but as always, large apertures are of advantage with their greater light grasp – which itself allows a higher magnification to be used – and their finer resolution.

The changes that occur on most of the planets mean that you never know what to expect when you go to the telescope. When you start observing don't be too disappointed by the tiny disks and the fact that you seem to see very little – it just takes a while for your eyes to 'learn' to make out faint details. As you get used to your equipment and have some practice, you will find that you see more and more. You will also find that there are tantalizing occasions when the seeing becomes perfect – usually for only too short a time – and the tiny disks are covered in so much detail that you have a difficult task in capturing the appearance in a drawing. Don't forget too, that it may be just as

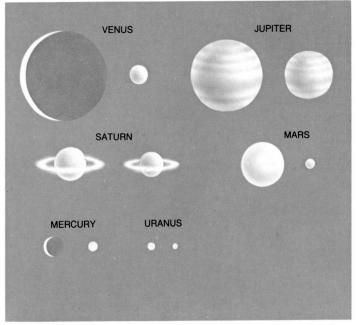

The maximum and minimum apparent sizes of the planets. Jupiter shows the least relative change.

important to know that no details were visible, as can sometimes happen, especially in the cases of Venus and Mars (pages 152 and 154), so always make a note of these 'negative' observations.

It does no harm just to look at the planets, and the more frequently you do this the more you are likely to see. Trying to make proper observations is even more satisfying, and it certainly helps you to become familiar with the planet's appearance. This is important as once you have gained that experience, anything unusual that happens will be immediately obvious.

Actual observations that you can carry out are: making whole-disk or detail drawings, estimating intensities and phases, and timing transits of features across the central meridians of the disks. (Photographic work tends to be so specialized that it is not considered here.) If you are a beginner you will probably want to start with whole-disk and detail drawings. Jupiter and Saturn offer the added attraction of various satellite phenomena, and these are discussed later (pages 163 and 165).

One point that deserves to be mentioned is that confusion can arise over the terms 'east' and 'west', when they are used to refer to planetary (and lunar) features. Before exploration by spacecraft became common, the usage was always applied in the same way as sky orientations (page 35), so that in the naked-eye view, a feature was east of another if it was to the left (as seen by a northern-hemisphere observer). However, with highly detailed spacecraft mapping (and to prevent confusion for astronauts on the Moon), it was obviously sensible for latitude and longitude to apply in the same way as on the Earth. This reversed the two directions east and west, and Mare Orientale ('Eastern Sea') is now west of the central meridian of the Moon.

Like the Moon, the planets have terminators dividing the illuminated from the unilluminated portions. In the cases of Mercury and Venus these are easily visible. With Mars it is more difficult, and Jupiter and Saturn are so distant from the Earth and the Sun that the terminators are, to all intents and purposes, the same as the visible limbs. The rotation of the planets gives rise to morning and evening terminators and in some cases this can be related to the appearance or occurrence of particular features (especially Martian clouds).

Planetary drawings

Before you can make planetary drawings you need suitable blank outlines. Even though the apparent planetary sizes may differ greatly around their orbits, particularly in the cases of Mars and Venus, most organizations which co-ordinate amateur work use fixed diameters for particular planets so that observations can be easily compared. Try to keep to these sizes if you draw any blanks for yourself.

There are some other points that have to be borne in mind. Both Jupiter and Saturn are considerably flattened by their rapid rotation, so their outlines are not perfectly circular, and you cannot use a pair of compasses. Their blanks have to be specially prepared by using a template or tracing from a proper outline (pages 161 and 164). Saturn, of course, has the added complication of the changing aspect of the rings. Mercury, Venus and Mars can be drawn with circular outlines, which helps, but they show phases, somewhat like the

Moon's, where part of the hemisphere turned towards Earth is not illuminated. With Mercury and usually in the case of Mars, the amount of phase can be accurately predicted, so you can draw it in advance. However, this does not apply to Venus (page 152), and the terminator must be added from actual observation. The amount of phase effect for Jupiter and Saturn is so small that it can be forgotten.

Just as you need some experience to be able to see the detail, so you need practice to show it in drawings. This is particularly the case with Mars, Jupiter and Saturn because of the amount of detail which they can show, and also because their rapid rotation means that the appearance changes during an observing session. You might find it better to start by trying to reproduce just the overall distribution of light and dark areas, or concentrating on some specific feature, rather than attempting fully-detailed, whole-disk drawings. As you gain experience, you can add more detail. In any case, as has been said before, it is probably as well to begin every drawing in this way.

Jupiter on 1983 July 19, 20:46 UT, drawn by Richard McKim, using a 216-mm (8″) reflector. Satellite Io is in transit in front of the northern component of the North Equatorial Belt and the North Tropical Zone.

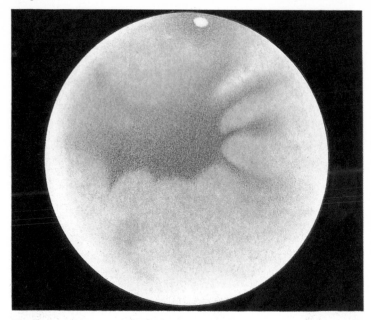

*This drawing of Mars was made by Richard Baum on 1973 October 30, using a 115-mm (4")
refractor at a magnification of 186.*

Intensity estimates

Generalized drawings can help to lead on to making intensity estimates. In
these, you assess particular features in terms of their relative brightness, and
give them numerical values. It is not as difficult as it sounds. The scale depends
upon the planet and the range of brightness which it shows, but normally a
value of 0 corresponds to white, and the numbers increase for darker features.
Unfortunately, but not surprisingly, there are usually differences between the
values that various observers give to the same feature. This also partly depends
upon the equipment that is used, including the magnification, as well as the
seeing conditions. There may be additional confusion over the exact
identifications, so it is a good idea if you give intensity estimates on an actual
drawing of the planet, even if it is only a rough sketch.

FILTERS   You can try the use of various filters to help in making ordinary
drawings or intensity estimates. However, unless your telescope is fairly large,
they may do more harm than good, because of the inevitable light losses that
they produce. Venus is the exception, as it may be so bright that a neutral-
density filter is useful in diminishing the glare, and thus making the details
more easily visible. Generally Mars and Venus are the most satisfactory
subjects for colour-filter observations, although there is no reason why they
should not be used on Jupiter and Saturn. On Mars, for example, a light blue
filter will accentuate atmospheric features, whereas one of an orange or

reddish tint might show greater surface detail. Some eyepieces are specially threaded so that optical glass filters can be screwed into place. These are ideal, but tend to be expensive. Ordinary photographic, gelatine filters cost much less and you can cut and mount them easily, either in simple holders or a special adaptor like that used for lunar filter observations (page 122). They are more delicate, however, and cannot be easily cleaned. Never mount any filters close to the objective's focal plane where any defects will be in focus and glaringly obvious. Photographs taken through filters of various colours make an interesting experiment.

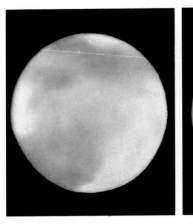
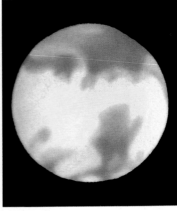

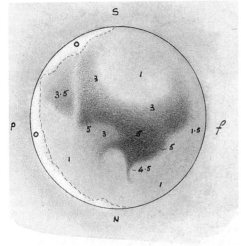

Above: *Mars as seen through blue (left) and red (right) filters, accentuating atmospheric and surface features respectively.*

Left: *An intensity diagram of Mars by Richard Baum, 1973 November 19, 22:30 UT.*

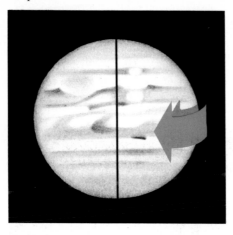

Either a real (crosswire) or imaginary central meridian may be used for planetary transit timings.

Transit timings

As a planet rotates, its various features are carried across the central meridian of the disk. The timing of these central meridian transits is a very valuable technique, even though it may not sound very appealing. You can use the times (accurate to about a minute), to find the actual longitudes of individual markings on the planets. Tables, given in the various handbooks, usually for both Mars and Jupiter, show the longitude of the central meridian at 00·00 UT, and how much it changes with particular intervals of time. From these you can easily establish the longitude of any feature that you observe. If you observe markings on more than one occasion the longitudes can be compared to see whether there has been any movement between the two observations. This is a very accurate method of recording the positions of planetary features. It is particularly fascinating to see the changes that take place on Jupiter, as some spots wander about and overtake others.

Another type of transit, that of the inferior planets across the Sun, is discussed on page 153.

Only spacecraft images can reveal details of the surface of Mercury.

The inferior planets

The two planets inside the orbit of the Earth (the inferior planets) are Mercury and Venus. Because of their orbits they show a full range of phases from the thinnest crescents, when they are at inferior conjunction between the Earth and the Sun (page 55), to 'full' phases at superior conjunction. As they are always close to the Sun, they never appear far above the horizon if you observe before sunrise or after sunset. For this reason observations are often made in actual daylight, usually in the period of about two hours after sunrise or before sunset, when the conditions are reasonably steady. In the case of Venus the reduced contrast between the planet and the background sky also means that more detail can then be seen.

Mercury

Mercury can reach about magnitude -1.7, not very different to Sirius (-1.4), but it is never more than about 28° from the Sun, so the first problem comes in locating it. If you live in the northern hemisphere it is easiest to find the planet at eastern elongations in the spring, and western elongations in the autumn, when it will appear highest, although its actual distance from the Sun can never be more than 18°. Greater elongations only occur when the planet is low in the sky. Conditions are best if you live in the southern hemisphere, as the planet can be both higher in the sky, and at its greatest elongation of about 28° in the morning in autumn or fall (April), and in the evening in spring (September) – at western and eastern elongations respectively. Observers in the tropics are generally well-placed to observe the planet at any elongation.

The only really satisfactory way of finding Mercury is by using setting circles (page 89), but as it is close to the Sun, always take great care, for safety's sake (page 139). When the planet is at eastern elongation, you can move so that the Sun is hidden behind a building. This is the only time when you can safely sweep for the planet, as the apparent motion of the Sun only puts you farther into shadow. Obviously the technique would not be safe for western elongations, but it is then easiest to find the object before sunrise. You can keep

---

Elongations of Mercury, 1985-2000

Western	Eastern
1985 Jan. 3, May 1, Aug. 28.	1985 Mar. 17, July 14, Nov. 8.
1986 Apr. 13, Aug. 11, Nov. 30.	1986 Feb. 28, June 25, Oct. 21.
1987 Mar. 26, July 25, Nov. 13.	1987 Feb. 12, June 7, Oct. 4.
1988 Mar. 8, July 6, Oct. 26.	1988 Jan. 26, May 19, Sept. 15.
1989 Feb. 18, June 18, Oct. 10.	1989 Jan. 9, May 1, Aug. 29 Dec. 23.
1990 Feb. 1, May 31, Sept. 24.	1990 Apr. 13, Aug. 11, Dec. 6.
1991 Jan. 14, May 12, Sept. 7, Dec. 27.	1991 Mar. 27, July 25, Nov. 19.
1992 Apr. 23, Aug. 21, Dec. 9.	1992 Mar. 9, July 6, Oct. 31.
1993 Apr. 5, Aug. 4, Nov. 22.	1993 Feb. 21, June 17, Oct. 14.
1994 Mar. 19, July 17, Nov. 6.	1994 Feb. 4, May 30, Sept. 26.
1995 Mar. 1, June 29, Oct. 20.	1995 Jan. 19, May 12, Sept. 9.
1996 Feb. 11, June 10, Oct. 3.	1996 Jan. 2, Apr. 23, Aug. 21, Dec. 15.
1997 Jan. 24, May 22, Sept. 16.	1997 Apr. 6, August. 4, Nov. 28.
1998 Jan. 6, May 4, Aug. 31, Dec. 20.	1998 Mar. 20, July 17, Nov. 11.
1999 Apr. 16, Aug. 14, Dec. 2.	1999 Mar. 3, June 28, Oct. 24.
2000 Mar. 28, July 27, Nov. 15.	2000 Feb. 15, June 9, Oct. 6.

track of the planet as it moves into the daylight sky ahead of the Sun.

Unfortunately once Mercury has been located there is little that can be observed. Its colour is often dull white, and this is most apparent when the more brilliant Venus is nearby in the sky, but it may also have a red or yellowish tinge. You will see the phases in a small telescope of about 75 mm aperture, but that is the most that is likely to be visible. Observers have distinguished some of the darkest markings with apertures of only 100–150 mm, but do not expect to see very much even with a very much larger telescope. It has been suggested that the details are somewhat easier to see if a pale yellow filter is used, and this is worth trying.

Venus

Venus is much more satisfactory, and being brighter (it can reach magnitude −4·3), it is usually much easier to find. Its elongation may reach 47°, when it is accessible for a few weeks. You will find that observations in daylight are the

Phenomena of Venus, 1985-2000			
E. Elongation	*Inferior Conjunction*	*W. Elongation*	*Superior Conjunction*
1985 Jan. 22	1985 Apr. 3	1985 June 13	1986 Jan. 19
1986 Aug. 27	1986 Nov. 5	1987 Jan. 15	1987 Aug. 23
1988 Apr. 3	1988 June 13	1988 Aug. 22	1989 Apr. 5
1989 Nov. 8	1990 Jan. 10	1990 Mar. 30	1990 Nov. 1
1991 June 13	1991 Aug. 22	1991 Nov. 2	1992 June 13
1993 Jan. 19	1993 Apr. 1	1993 June 10	1994 Jan. 17
1994 Aug. 25	1994 Nov. 2	1995 Jan. 13	1995 Aug. 20
1996 Apr. 1	1996 June 10	1996 Aug. 19	1997 Apr. 2
1997 Nov. 6	1998 Jan. 16	1998 Mar. 27	1998 Oct. 30
1999 June 11	1999 Aug. 20	1999 Oct. 30	2000 June 11

most satisfactory as the glare is considerably reduced, allowing the faint details to be seen. If you use a telescope you may still need a neutral–density filter to diminish the amount of light from the planet. Venus is larger than Mercury, and comes closer to the Earth, so you can even see the phases with good binoculars. To make out any details you still need apertures of at least 100 mm, and preferably more.

The only details visible are those of the uppermost layer of clouds in the dense atmosphere, so they are, at best, ill-defined and rather difficult to draw. However, it should be remembered that amateur observations of these faint markings obtained a rotational period for the upper atmosphere of about four days well before this was confirmed by spacecraft measurements. (The 243-day rotation of the invisible solid body of Venus is retrograde.)

You may see both light and dark markings on the disk, but it is frequently difficult to show these in any drawing without exaggerating the contrast. Make a note if you find that this is necessary. If possible, make proper intensity estimates at the same time. Bright 'cusp-caps' are frequently recorded, generally, but not always precisely, over the polar regions. Apparently darker 'collars' around these caps are sometimes visible. A filter can help to accentuate the details on Venus and a light yellow (Wratten 15) is the best to try. As always it is still important to make a note when there is no visible detail.

The horns of the crescent may sometimes appear unequal, being either blunted or extended. The terminator can also be irregular, rather than a smooth curve. Try to record these changes in a careful drawing. The irregularities on the terminator can make it more difficult to determine the planet's apparent phase, which generally differs from the one predicted. In particular at half-phase, or **dichotomy**, the discrepancy may amount to several days. (This is known as the Schröter Effect, after the observer who first noted it.) Dichotomy is early at eastern elongations, and late at western ones. Although this effect is definitely real, no cause has yet been established. Because the terminator position is not easy to record, several drawings are really required from each observing session, so that an average value of the

Even with careful use of filters, photographs of Venus from Earth only rarely hint at atmospheric details.

observed phase can be deduced. A micrometer is the most accurate method of obtaining these results, but unfortunately very few observers have one.

Another uncertain effect is that of the 'Ashen Light'. When the crescent is very narrow, the dark portion of the disk may appear to be faintly luminous. The only chance of seeing this effect is if you can fit an eyepiece with a home-made, occulting bar, shaped to hide the bright crescent. Although it has been suggested that perhaps some auroral phenomenon might be involved, it is still possible that it is just an optical illusion, like the opposite effect where the unlimited side of Venus appears to be darker than the surrounding sky.

Transits

Mercury and Venus occasionally cross the disk of the Sun. These events, known as transits, must be observed with safe methods like those used for studying solar features (page 139). Transits of Mercury are more frequent than those of Venus and will occur on 1986 November 13, 1993 November 6, and 1999 November 15. Venus transits occur in pairs with more than a century between each pair. The last transits were in December 1874 and December 1882: the next will be in June 2004 and June 2012.

Mars

Mars is a wonderful object to study, so it is a great pity that it is not favourably placed every year. Oppositions are about 780 days apart, and when these occur near aphelion (in January and Feburary) the apparent diameter may be as small as 13″. It can rise to nearly 26″ at oppositions near perihelion (in August and September). Anyone living in the southern hemisphere has a wonderful opportunity at these oppositions, as Mars is then south of the ecliptic, and very low for observers north of the equator. The south pole of Mars is turned towards the Earth on these occasions, the north pole only being visible when Mars is around aphelion. Despite the difficulties, good observers can still see a lot of detail at most oppositions.

There are numerous dark markings on the lighter background of the disk. As the planet rotates and different longitudes come into view, new features slowly become visible from night to night. With patience, a map can be built up, showing the appearance right round the planet. Most of the markings are definitely permanent, and are seen at every apparition. Others show changes when observed over a period of years. For a long time it was thought that these alterations might be due to vegetation, but we now know that the winds move material from one area, depositing it in another. Dust storms sometimes completely obliterate the dark markings over the whole of the planetary surface, particularly at perihelic oppositions. It is then interesting to watch the features, perhaps changed in outline or intensity, gradually reappear as the veil of dust subsides. Lesser storms may affect individual regions of the surfaces. These dust storms are the 'yellow hazes' mentioned by earlier observers.

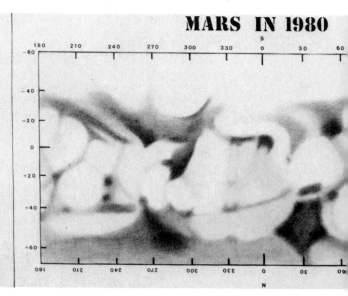

The brilliant polar caps wax and wane with the Martian seasons, and the southern cap may even disappear completely. Portions may become detached before they gradually dwindle away, and other rifts are sometimes visible. The darker collars surrounding the caps do not appear to be entirely due to contrast effects, and changes in the covering of dust are probably involved. Frequently, however, the features in the polar regions are masked by a 'polar hood' of cloud, which may sometimes extend over 50-60° of latitude. This cloud tends to disperse at mid-winter, when it is frozen out onto the surface, but reappears in the spring as the warmth of the Sun increases, turning the ice back into vapour. We now know that the permanent northern cap is ordinary water ice, but that the seasonal caps consist of both water and carbon dioxide. The latter only freezes during the coldest part of the winter.

Other whitish 'hazes', are sometimes visible elsewhere on Mars, most particularly at the morning terminator, where clouds formed during the night have not yet dispersed. But they are not confined to just this region, and some can be followed as they move across the surface. Other 'blue hazes' can cover very considerable areas of the disk.

Observing Mars

Once again you really need an aperture of at least 100 mm to be able to see any proper details of the surface, and 150 mm would be better for regular observation. Magnifications of 200-400 are likely to be the most satisfactory.

The positions of the major dark features are fairly well-established, but good drawings of individual markings are always of interest. However, try to make at least one or two whole-disk drawings at each apparition. Despite the

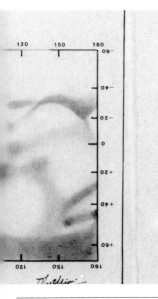

Left: *A map of Mars prepared by Richard McKim from observations made in 1980.*

Below: *Mars by Richard Baum, 1980 February 17, 22:40 UT, showing a large amount of cloud on the morning limb.*

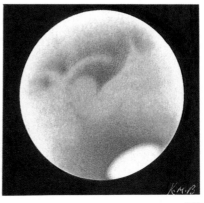

Oppositions of Mars, 1986-2000

Date of Opposition	Closest Approach to Earth	Apparent diameter "	Magnitude	Constellation
1986 July 10	1986 July 16	23·1	−2·4	Sagittarius
1988 Sept. 28	1988 Sept. 22	23·7	−2·6	Pisces
1990 Nov. 27	1990 Nov. 20	17·9	−1·7	Taurus
1993 Jan. 7	1993 Jan. 3	14·9	−1·2	Gemini
1995 Feb. 12	1995 Feb. 11	13·8	−1·0	Leo
1997 Mar. 17	1997 Mar. 20	14·2	−1·1	Virgo
1999 Apr. 24	1999 May 1	16·2	−1·5	Virgo

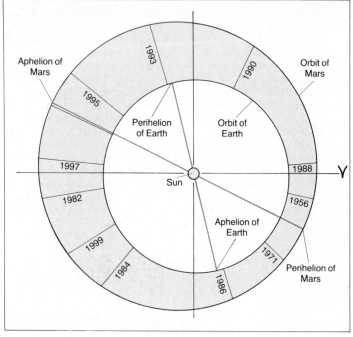

considerable changes in the diameter of the planet it is probably best to use always a single size of observing blank that is 2 inches (51 mm) in diameter. The phase may amount to as much as 46° and so needs to be accurately reproduced. You can find details of the phase at any time in one of the astronomical yearbooks.

As Mars rotates fairly rapidly, you should not take too long in making a detailed, whole-disk drawing. Start by locating the polar cap, but remember that this may not be centred precisely on the pole. (The position of the poles depends upon the exact tilt of the axis as seen from Earth, but once again, a yearbook will give you that information.) Next, sketch the most prominent dark features, and make a note of the time when you finish this basic drawing. You can then carry on, adding the finer details and outlining the brighter areas.

A light blue filter is very useful for showing atmospheric features, and a Wratten 44B is recommended. Although other, strongly-coloured filters have often been suggested in the past, they are only suitable for experienced observers using large instruments. In most small telescopes, Mars does not appear highly coloured, due to the limited light-grasp, and dense filters will only degrade the image, rather than enhance it.

INTENSITY ESTIMATES   Intensity estimates (page 148) are very valuable, and should be attempted. Like many other astronomical observing techniques, they are not that difficult after a little practice. Use a scale running from 0 (brightest) to 10. The polar caps are usually taken as intensity 0, and a black sky background as 10. The latter in particular, however, does depend upon the equipment and magnification being used. The sketch accompanying the intensity estimates can be quite rough and 'unfinished' provided the features are easily identifiable.

TRANSIT TIMINGS   You can also try making central meridian timings (page 150). A little practice soon enables you to judge when a feature is exactly half-way across the disk. Don't try to make lots of timings of very faint details, as these may be difficult to identify. The bolder, more distinct features are far better. In any case, timings can only be carried out when Mars appears 'full'. This is only for about 7-10 days each side of opposition. At other times the phase makes the task impossible.

PHOTOGRAPHY   Photography of Mars really requires large apertures and long focal lengths to give reasonably-sized, bright images. In recent years, some amateurs with large telescopes, by perseverance, and by making the most of occasions of exceptionally good seeing, have managed to secure some excellent pictures of the planet. Although these have usually been with black-and-white films, sometimes exposed through different filters, some success has been achieved with colour films.

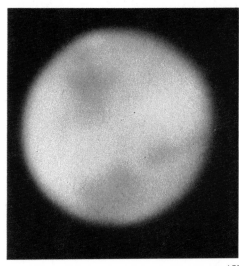

Left: *Some years are more favourable than others for observing Mars.*

Right: *Successful photography of Mars is very difficult and requires great experience and perseverance.*

Minor planets

Most amateurs find that the main challenge in observing minor planets (or asteroids as they are quite frequently called) comes in locating and following them. Most of the orbits lie between those of Mars and Jupiter, and they are all quite small – the three largest being Ceres, diameter 1000 km (620 miles), and Pallas and Vesta, both with diameters of about 540 km (330 miles). They are faint; only Vesta can rise to just about the naked-eye limit and perhaps half-a-dozen others may exceed magnitude 10 at opposition. Nevertheless there is a considerable sense of achievement in managing to track one down from the details given in the yearly handbooks, and even more in keeping it in view for a period of time. The best way of doing this is undoubtedly to plot the positions on charts which show stars fainter than the objects' expected magnitudes.

Left: *The minor planet Eros passing close to κ Geminorum on 1975 January 24. An occultation was predicted, but was not observed.*

Right: *A minor planet may be identified either by its motion from night to night (a, b, c) or by its trail during an exposure (d).*

Photography

Photography can be attempted with any driven equipment, and depending upon the minor planet's position in its orbit should show the motion on exposures taken on different nights. Obviously this may not be the case if it is near one of its stationary points (page 54). Although there is no reason why 35-mm cameras should not be used, better results will generally be obtained with those that use larger film sizes, while still giving a fairly wide field of view. The objects that come close to the Earth, or cross its orbit, may sometimes move so rapidly that they can be recorded as trails. Good quality photographs can be used to obtain positions, and thus refine the orbits of some of the poorly-known minor planets, but these generally require special attention to equipment and methods.

Some minor planets show changes in brightness, due to the fact that they are irregularly shaped and rotating. The magnitudes can be estimated by the methods generally used for variable stars (page 174), but unfortunately it is usually very difficult to obtain satisfactory magnitudes of comparison stars. Photographs of the surrounding star fields taken through the appropriate filters (page 103) can be of help here, but most progress is likely to be made by those dedicated amateur astronomers who have photoelectric equipment.

Occultations

One fascinating field is that of occultations, predictions for which have become possible in recent years. The methods used are like those for lunar grazing occultations (page 138), and similar occultation tracks can be prepared. If the star is brighter than the minor planet, use a small telescope so that the latter remains invisible. The star will suddenly vanish and reappear, and there will be no confusion from the two images merging as can happen with a larger aperture.

There are considerable errors in the orbital information for many objects and also in many stellar positions, so last-minute checks have to be made by the professional astronomers engaged in this work to refine the predictions. A change of hundreds of kilometres may be produced by only small errors. Amateurs are frequently able to move to another observing site to compensate for this. The information gained from accurate timing gives the most precise measurements of the sizes of minor planets, and in some cases their individual shape. Possible satellite bodies have also been recorded.

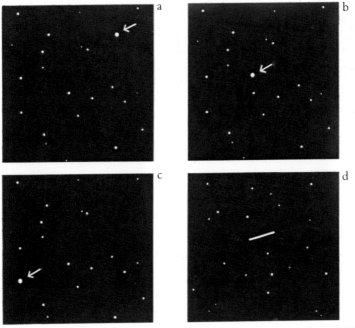

Jupiter

Jupiter is probably the most fascinating of the planets to observe. It is one of the four 'gas giants' – Saturn, Uranus and Neptune are the others – and mainly consists of the light elements hydrogen and helium. Jupiter's visible markings occur in the uppermost layers of its deep atmosphere, which contains many other gases, including methane and ammonia. There are both large-scale markings, and many smaller features that are always changing. If you only have a small telescope of about 50 mm in diameter, you will still be able to see that the disk is divided into dark belts and polar regions, and brighter zones. But even these major features are by no means permanent, as they strengthen and fade,

Left: *Jupiter, photographed from Earth, showing atmospheric features, a satellite and shadow transits.*

Below: *Voyager observations showed the Great Red Spot to be a long-lasting atmospheric storm.*

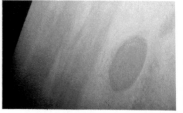

and divide into more than one component. Apertures of 150 mm or more are really needed to show some of the vast amount of tiny detail on the various parts of the disk.

The markings are generally referred to as light and dark 'spots', although 'festoons', 'plumes' and 'ovals' are some of the other terms used from time to time. All these, as well as generally darker and lighter regions, can be followed as they are carried round the planet, sometimes speeding up or slowing down as they change their positions in the atmosphere. Some of the tiny markings may be seen for only a few days before they fade and disappear. The famous Great Red Spot has probably persisted for hundreds of years, but not without changes. Its position can usually be seen in most amateur-sized telescopes, but do not be too disappointed if you find it without the vivid coloration of some photographs and spacecraft images.

One of the advantages that Jupiter offers is that oppositions occur at intervals of about 13 months (roughly twice as often as those of Mars), and allow several weeks of observation. Jupiter, too, is unlike Mars in that its apparent size does not vary greatly. Its phase and tilt are negligible, so that when you are making sketches you do not have to worry about these details. Only if you are preparing outline blanks for whole-disk drawings must you take its flattening into account. The large size of Jupiter also makes it an ideal subject for planetary photography.

Jupiter's rotation is fast – it is the cause of the considerable flattening – and in

Oppositions of Jupiter, 1985-2000

Year and date	Diameter secs. of arc	Magnitude	Year and date	Diameter secs. of arc	Magnitude
1985 Aug. 4	48·5	−2·3	1994 Apr. 30	44·5	−2·0
1986 Sept. 10	49·6	−2·4	1995 June 1	45·6	−2·1
1987 Oct. 18	49·8	−2·5	1996 July 4	47·0	−2·2
1988 Nov. 23	48·7	−2·4	1997 Aug. 9	48·6	−2·4
1989 Dec. 27	47·2	−2·3	1998 Sept. 16	49·7	−2·5
1991 Jan. 28	45·7	−2·1	1999 Oct. 23	49·8	−2·5
1992 Feb. 28	44·6	−2·0	2000 Nov. 28	48·5	−2·4
1993 Mar. 30	44·2	−2·0			

the deep interior amounts to about 9 hours 55 minutes 30 seconds. But the deep atmosphere and highly complicated meteorology mean that the atmospheric layers rotate at rather different speeds. The apparent 'day' amounts to about 9 hours, 50 minutes 30 seconds in the equatorial region and 9 hours 55 minutes 40 seconds for the rest of the planet. The two visible divisions, and the two periods,

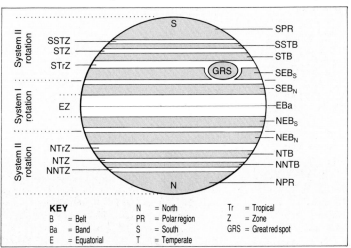

The belts, zones and other features that may be observed on Jupiter.

are known as System I and System II respectively. The yearly handbooks give tables showing the longitudes, in both of these Systems, for the centre of the disk at any date and time.

There is so much detail on Jupiter when viewed through a moderate-sized telescope, that it really is best to start by making sketches of individual features. The rotation periods of Jupiter are such that a different region is visible at the same time each night. The rotation is so fast that many observers have developed the technique of drawing 'strip-sketches'. These show just one or two particular belts and zones around the planet, the various markings being recorded as the rotation brings them into view.

It is certainly worth attempting to make whole-disk drawings from time to time, as these then show the general aspect of the planet, which can change considerably from one apparition to the next. When you start observing, don't attempt to include too much detail on whole-disk drawings, as you only have 10 minutes at the very most to complete the sketch before the rotation changes the appearance. Concentrate on showing the relative strength of the belts and zones. Just as with the other planets, intensity estimates (page 148) are very useful in deciding the prominence of the various regions.

Jupiter, with its wealth of markings, is the best subject for central meridian transit timings. Simply record the times (to an accuracy of one minute) when features appear exactly in the centre of the disk. You can then work out the precise longitude of any feature quite easily by using the published tables. You only have to make sure that you can recognise the correct System to which a particular belt belongs. Sometimes this is a little difficult to decide when markings are on the borders of the two regions, but if in doubt, calculate and record both longitudes. If a feature is observed more than once the longitudes can be compared, and a plot will show you how the markings change their positions over a period of time, overtaking one another as they are carried round the planet.

The most prominent feature, the Great Red Spot, is no exception to the general drift in longitude, and has been followed many times completely 'around' the planet. Its size, prominence, and colour are all subject to change, and it appears to have been gradually fading and shrinking over the years.

Dark plumes cross the Equatorial Zone in a drawing (below left) of Jupiter on 1983 June 18. The photograph (below right), taken on 1983 July 2, shows their shift with respect to the Great Red Spot.

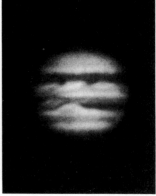

Jupiter's satellites

Jupiter's four major satellites are Io, Europa, Ganymede and Callisto. They have been known since Galileo first turned his primitive telescope onto the planet. (To this day they are frequently called the 'Galilean satellites'.) They are visible with even the smallest binoculars, and it is said that they may be visible to the naked eye, especially to an observer in the tropics where the planet may be overhead. They weave a complex pattern around Jupiter, and it is only on rare occasions that all four may appear to be 'missing'.

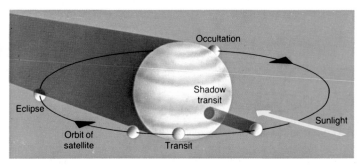

Above: *How the various phenomena of Jupiter's satellites occur.*

Apertures of 50–75 mm are enough to show various interesting events as they pass in front of, and behind the planet. Their shadows can be seen, as well as the transits of the bodies themselves. They are eclipsed by Jupiter's shadow and occulted by the body of the planet. What is more, every six years, when their orbital plane is aligned with the Earth, they also affect one another in the same way. These satellite phenomena are fascinating to watch, and should be timed as accurately as possible. Although no detail can be seen on any of the satellites with even very large telescopes, the difference in their appearance is quite striking when they are seen against the disk of the planet.

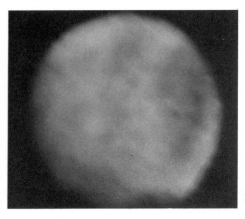

This distant Voyager image of Ganymede shows more detail than ever seen from Earth.

Saturn

With its spectacular system of rings, Saturn is as striking an object to observe as Jupiter. The methods used are essentially the same, although Saturn only rarely shows distinct markings, apart from the belts and zones. This is partly due to its greater distance, but we now know that a high atmospheric haze hides the features in the lower cloud layers. This makes it all the more important to follow the various light and dark spots that do occasionally arise.

Saturn's oppositions are separated by intervals of about 378 days. Although the phase is small, amounting to no more than 6° at the most, the most obvious variation comes in the tilt of the rings (and of the planet, of course). Twice in a Saturnian year (once every 15 years), the Earth passes through the plane of the rings. The rings are extremely thin, with an average thickness of possibly less than 100 metres (about 110 yards), and when this occurs they may temporarily disappear. Gradually one hemisphere comes more into view, whilst the rings begin to hide the other, until the tilt reaches its maximum value of about 28°. Then the change reverses direction, until the Earth is again in the ring-plane, after which the other hemisphere is fully exposed. The last passage of the ring-plane was in 1980, and the next is in 1995. This constantly changing aspect, together with the planet's very appreciable polar flattening, means that the preparation of blanks for drawings is very complicated. You will probably find it best to obtain master blanks from one of the amateur observational organisations.

Oppositions of Saturn, 1985-2000

Date	Magnitude	Date	Magnitude
1985 May 15	+0·2	1993 Aug. 19	+0·5
1986 May 27	+0·2	1994 Sept. 1	+0·7
1987 June 9	+0·2	1995 Sept. 14	+0·8
1988 June 20	+0·2	1996 Sept. 26	+0·7
1989 July 2	+0·2	1997 Oct. 10	+0·4
1990 July 14	+0·3	1998 Oct. 23	+0·2
1991 July 26	+0·3	1999 Nov. 6	0·0
1992 Aug. 7	+0·4	2000 Nov. 19	−0·1

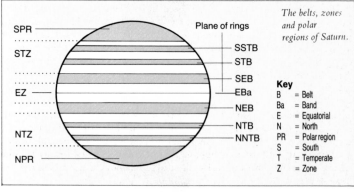

The belts, zones and polar regions of Saturn.

SPR — Plane of rings
STZ
SSTB
STB
SEB
EZ
EBa
NEB
NTB
NTZ
NNTB
NPR

Key
B = Belt
Ba = Band
E = Equatorial
N = North
PR = Polar region
S = South
T = Temperate
Z = Zone

Above: *Saturn on 1982 April 21, 21:00 UT, with a large – 320 mm (12″) – refractor, at magnifications of 230 and 320.*

Above right: *This photograph of Saturn shows how it is fairly featureless when compared with Jupiter.*

Left: *This Voyager image shows many ringlets within the outer (divided) Ring A, wide Ring B and the fainter Ring C, as well as the shadow of the rings on the body of the planet.*

The rings of Saturn

The main portions of the rings: the outer, reasonably bright Ring A; the even brighter Ring B; and the Cassini Division between them are easy to see. Ring C, the innermost, is not so readily visible, and its transparent nature gave rise to its alternative name of the Crêpe Ring. When viewed against the disk it sometimes looks very similar to a dusky belt. Frequently the shadow of the planet obscures a portion of the rings, and they may appear dark against the disk when, near the dates of ring-plane passage, the Sun and Earth are on opposite sides of their plane. Various irregularities are reported from time to time, and should be carefully drawn.

Satellites

Again like Jupiter, Saturn has an interesting set of satellites, the brightest, Titan, being of magnitude 8. Three more are brighter than 10·5, and yet a further three over 12·1. When the Earth passes through their orbital plane they may appear as bright beads of light strung on the thin line of the rings. In large telescopes, satellite phenomena like those of the Galilean satellites of Jupiter are then visible.

The outer planets

Unfortunately the outer planets do not give very much scope for observation, but they do offer the challenge of locating and following them. Uranus and Neptune are reasonably bright at opposition (reaching maximum magnitudes of around 5·6 and 7·7 respectively). They are not too difficult to find in small telescopes, using suitable charts and ephemerides. They slowly work their way eastwards against the stars, Uranus increasing its RA by about 20 minutes per year, and Neptune by about half that amount. Both are at present in the southern part of the ecliptic (in the constellations of Ophiuchus and Sagittarius respectively), Neptune in particular being rather more difficult to locate amongst the star clouds of the Milky Way.

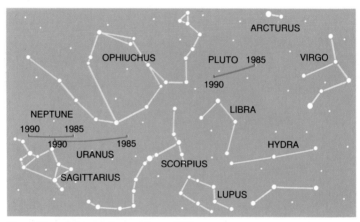

The positions of the outer planets to the year 1990.

Uranus

Uranus is distinctly different from stars in appearance, and shows a minute disk in a good telescope, which may be seen as bluish or greenish depending on the observer's eyesight. Faint belts and zones have been recorded by people using

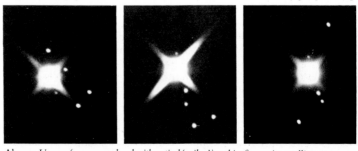

Above: *Uranus (overexposed and with optical 'spikes') and its five major satellites.*

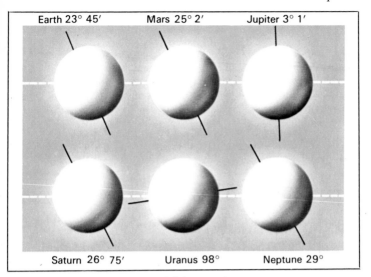

Earth 23° 45'   Mars 25° 2'   Jupiter 3° 1'

Saturn 26° 75'   Uranus 98°   Neptune 29°

Uranus has the greatest axial inclination of all the major planets.

very large telescopes, but there are no obvious, definite markings. The planet is very unusual as its axis of rotation is nearly in the orbital plane, being tilted by about 98°, so that at times (in 1986 for example) the polar regions are presented to the Earth. When this happens little detail can be expected.

Neptune

Neptune shows no detail in amateur telescopes. Both Uranus and Neptune have been suspected of showing some changes in magnitude over a very long period of time. There have been suggestions that variations might be related to solar activity, but this remains quite uncertain. The magnitudes of both planets could be estimated quite easily by variable star methods (page 174).

Pluto

Pluto, the planet with the greatest average distance from the Sun – its eccentric orbit has brought it inside the orbit of Neptune at present – is very difficult to locate with most amateur telescopes. The magnitude is about 14, so apertures of about 300 mm are required for it to be visible at all. Being so faint, Pluto can be easily confused with the surrounding stars, and the best method of locating it is by means of photography on different dates. Charts are published in some of the astronomical yearbooks. At present the yearly motion is similar to that of Neptune, being actually slightly greater as the planet is marginally closer to the Sun.

Pluto is now very much farther away from the ecliptic than Uranus and Neptune, due to its high orbital inclination. Brightness changes are thought to occur as the planet approaches and recedes from the Sun, but the period is so long (about 250 years), that despite Pluto having been discovered in 1930, there is still very little known about the planet.

Comets

Comets are often referred to as 'dirty snowballs'. As far as we know they are basically very small bodies only a few kilometres across, consisting of ices and dust particles. They remain invisible until their elongated orbits bring them into the centre of the Solar System, where the heat of the Sun causes some of the ices to evaporate as various gases. Some comets may then become spectacular objects.

The parts of a comet. The gas tail always points away from the Sun, but the dust tail spreads behind the comet in its orbit.

Never miss the opportunity to observe a bright comet. Although several are usually visible in a year to amateurs with moderate-sized equipment, most of those that are regular visitors to the inner Solar System are very faint. The only exception is Halley's Comet, which normally becomes quite prominent each time it returns in its 76-year orbit. The really spectacular comets are the unexpected ones, which can suddenly arrive from almost any direction, and which may be approaching the Sun for the very first time. There are then a few hectic weeks for cometary astronomers, whilst the bright comet swings round the Sun, before disappearing again into the distance, perhaps only to return in thousands of years' time. On rare occasions, and especially when a comet has passed close to the Sun, it may fragment, each portion appearing as a comet in its own right.

The appearance of comets can vary greatly. All show a head (the **coma**) which may never appear as more than a fuzzy patch, even when the comet is closest to the Sun. Others may show distinct features, the most notable of which is the tail. This usually becomes more conspicuous as the comet nears perihelion and the increasing heat of the Sun releases both gases and dust from the icy cometary body. Some comets show two tails: one curved and formed of dust particles, and the other straight, gaseous, and pointing directly away from the Sun. A few cases of multiple (dust) tails are also known, and tails have been recorded as stretching half-way across the sky. The dust from comets is thought to give rise to most of the tiny particles that are observed as meteors (page 113) and which form the zodiacal light (page 108).

Within the coma, a tiny, bright, star-like point (the **nucleus**) is sometimes visible, and this looks the same even with the highest magnification. Do not confuse it with the structure that you may sometimes see in the coma itself, and which appears as shells or jets of material.

Observing comets

You can use any equipment for observation, and may sometimes find that the great extent of tail is revealed by the naked eye, binoculars, or very wide-field telescopes. Large apertures and magnifications are required, however, to see the intricate detail near the nucleus. With any equipment, make drawings in ways similar to those used for rendering the planets (page 94). It is also worth trying some photography. This will record both the actual position of the head, and may capture the tail or some of its structure when it is too faint to be seen by other means. Wide-field, fast lenses are required for this work, while telescopes or long-focus cameras are needed to record details of the coma. To obtain the best results the equipment should be guided to follow the motion of the comet itself, when the background stars will show as trails. Short-focus lenses may be driven to follow the stars.

Many advanced amateurs undertake comet searches, but this requires an immense degree of patience to learn the star patterns and possible confusing objects such as clusters and galaxies over a large area of the sky. Wide-field, large binoculars or short-focus telescopes are normally employed for this sort of work, and searches are often carried out in the region near the Sun where a comet may approach very close to the Sun and Earth without being detected.

Comet Humason, observed in 1962, had a very irregular coma and tail.

Stars

The colours of stars are an approximate indication of the temperatures of their visible surfaces. These temperatures range from about 40 000°C (about 72 000°F) for rare blue–white stars like ζ Orionis down to about 3000°C (about 5400°F) for a deep red star such as μ Cephei, the famous 'Garnet Star'. There

Coloured stars

Star	Name	Colour
α Aur	Capella	Yellow
α Boo	Arcturus	Orange-yellow
α CMa	Sirius	Blue white
μ Cep	'Garnet Star'	Deep red
α Lyr	Vega	Blue-white
α Sco	Antares	Red
α Tau	Aldebaran	Orange

are even rare examples beyond these two extremes. Some interesting coloured stars are given in the table, but some observers may have difficulty in seeing the tints as much depends on the equipment and the observer's eyesight. At low light levels colours are not readily visible to the eye although distinct on photographs. Greater apertures make them more apparent. In addition various observers have completely different responses, some being blue-sensitive and having difficulty with red stars, and others finding the opposite. Generally red stars seem to become brighter and brighter the longer they are observed. (This is a problem with some variable star observations.) Double stars (page 179) often show striking colour combinations, mainly due to the effect of contrast.

Below left: *Taurus and part of Orion, a five-minute exposure taken with a driven camera and a 50-mm (2″) lens.*

Below right: *The magnitudes of stars in Ursa Minor and Crux are useful guides to magnitudes elsewhere in the sky.*

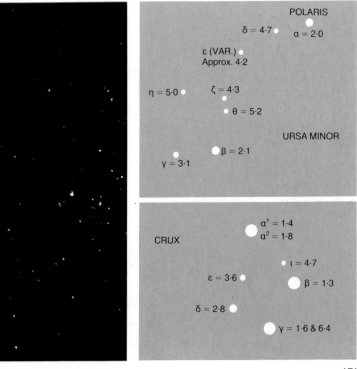

POLARIS
$\delta = 4\cdot7$ $\alpha = 2\cdot0$

ε (VAR.)
Approx. $4\cdot2$

$\eta = 5\cdot0$ $\zeta = 4\cdot3$

$\theta = 5\cdot2$

URSA MINOR

$\beta = 2\cdot1$

$\gamma = 3\cdot1$

CRUX

$\alpha^1 = 1\cdot4$
$\alpha^2 = 1\cdot8$

$\iota = 4\cdot7$

$\varepsilon = 3\cdot6$ $\beta = 1\cdot3$

$\delta = 2\cdot8$

$\gamma = 1\cdot6$ & $6\cdot4$

Temperature: 25,000°C	11,000°C	6,000°C	4,000°C	3,000°C
Typical star: Spica	Sirius	Sun	Arcturus	Betelgeuse

The colours and temperatures of some bright, well-known stars.

Spectral classes

Catalogues frequently list the spectral classes of individual stars. This is a more scientific method of describing temperature and composition, defined on the basis of which elements cause the lines visible in the spectrum of a particular star. The classes, arranged from hottest to coolest, follow the now rather jumbled sequence O, B, A, F, G, K, M. (The usual mnemonic is 'Oh Be A Fine Girl Kiss Me'.) The rarer classes R, N, S, C, WN, and WC may be mentioned at times. Each class has 10 main subdivisions, numbered 0–9 (hottest to coolest) and the overall range in stars is from about O5 to M8. The Sun is a G2 star, surface temperature about 6000°C (about 11000°F).

Stars are also described on the basis of their sizes and luminous output. They range from supergiant stars like α Scorpii (Antares), larger than the orbit of Mars, to tiny white dwarfs smaller than the Earth.

Magnitudes and distances of stars

To the eye a star of first magnitude appears twice as bright as one of second magnitude, which in turn appears twice as bright as one of third magnitude. Actually they are not; each magnitude interval is slightly brighter than that amount, the true ratio being 2·512:1. The eye and brain perceive that constant *ratio* as a constant *step*. For most purposes we can forget the mathematical relationship, although it is easy to remember that a first magnitude star is exactly 100 times the brightness of a star of sixth magnitude. It is sometimes helpful to know the magnitudes of some of the brightest stars, and these are given in the table. The very brightest have negative magnitudes. Some exact, fainter magnitudes are given in the small charts for Ursa Minor, Crux and the Pleiades.

The distances of stars are very difficult to measure (even nowadays). They are so great that kilometres and even astronomical units (page 141) are inconvenient, so astronomers use either light-years, or for preference, **parsecs** (pc). One parsec (*parallax second*) is that distance at which the radius of the Earth's orbit, 1 astronomical unit, subtends an angle of 1 second of arc. It is

3·216 light–years, 206 265 astronomical units or about 31 million million km. Kiloparsecs (kpc: 1000 parsecs) and Megaparsecs (Mpc: 1 000 000 parsecs) are also used for galactic and extragalactic distances.

The magnitudes mentioned already – those that we see from the Earth – are **apparent magnitudes** (m). But stars differ greatly in their actual brightness and an apparently bright star may be a brilliant one far away, or a faint one near at hand. So the brightness of stars (the **luminosity**) has to be reduced to a standard distance. This has been chosen as 10 parsecs, and the magnitudes are known as **absolute magnitudes** (M). The difference between the two types of magnitude can be very striking and a few notable examples are given in the table.

Apparent/Absolute magnitudes

	m	M
α Boo	−0.06	−0.2
α CMa	−1.45	+1.41
α Cen	−0.10	+4.3
β Cen	0.60	−5.0
α Cyg	1.25	−7.3
α Ori	0.80	−6.0
β Ori	0.11	−7.0
α Sco	1.0	−4.7
Sun	−26.8	+4.79

Variable stars

Many stars are variables and show changes in their brightness. A plot of a star's apparent magnitude against time produces a **light–curve**, and this can give a lot of information about the star itself. Depending upon the type of object the changes may take place in just a few minutes or over a period of many years. The most obvious cause of variation is when stars are part of a binary system (page 177), where the orbital plane is aligned with the Earth, so that the two stars occasionally eclipse one another. Algol (β Persei) is the most famous example of this class, ranging between about magnitudes 2·2 and 3·4. In some cases both primary and secondary minima are observed, as the bright and faint components, respectively, are eclipsed.

Apart from these eclipsing systems there are many other types of variables, some of which are close binary systems and others are single stars. Many of the different forms of variation (and light curves) are linked with particular stages of stellar evolution. For amateur astronomers the most important types are probably the long–period variables (LPV), semiregulars (SR) and various eruptives (which include some showing sudden fades rather than outbursts). There are so many variable stars, of all magnitudes, that their study is one of the most satisfying fields of research for amateurs.

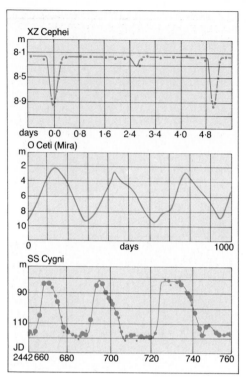

Top: *This eclipsing binary light-curve is drawn from single observations (dots). Centre: The averages from many individual observations are used to construct the smooth light-curve of a long-period variable. Bottom: The size of the dots gives an indication of the number of observations used at each point in this light-curve of an eruptive variable.*

Right: *A chart (with comparison star designations and magnitudes) for the semi-regular variable AC Herculis.*

Estimating magnitudes

It is not difficult to estimate the magnitudes of variable stars. You need to have the magnitudes of comparison stars and can obtain these on special charts issued by variable star organizations, frequently with additional 'finder' charts to help in locating the variable. Once you have found the star field, see if the variable is visible. If not, make a note of the faintest comparison star that you can see, and write down 'not visible, below . . .' Even that information is helpful. If the star is visible, decide which of the comparison stars seems slightly brighter and which seems fainter. If the variable appears exactly the same as one of them, check the next brighter or fainter as well. It is usually quite easy to get this far, and you have already roughly determined the star's magnitude.

Try using the 'fractional method' to take it further. Look at the three stars again. Is the variable half-way between the others in brightness? If so, write down 'A(1)V(1)B', where A and B are the bright and faint comparisons, respectively. 'V' is entered for the variable (whatever its actual name may be), and the figures represent the fractions – exactly the same in this case. The sequence is always 'bright star, fraction, variable, fraction, faint star'. Does the variable seem one third of the way from one to the other? Then write

Variable stars

Desig.	RA		Dec.		Range (mag)	Type	Remarks
	h	m	°				
R And	00	24	+38	35	6.9 – 14.3	LPV	
R Car	09	32	−62	47	3.9 – 10.0	LPV	
ρ Cas	23	54	+57	30	4.1 – 6.2	RCB?	
δ Cep	22	29	+58	26	3.9 – 5.0	Cep.	Pulsating star
o Cet	02	19	−02	58	3.5 – 9.1	LPV	'Mira'
R CrB	15	49	+28	10	5.8 – 14.8	RCB	Irregular fades
SS Cyg	21	43	+43	35	8.2 – 12.4	UG	Eruptive star
χ Cyg	19	51	+32	55	5.2 – 13.4	LPV	
AC Her	18	30	+21	52	7.0 – 8.4	RV	Minima alter
R Leo	09	48	+11	26	4.4 – 11.3	LPV	
U Mon	07	31	−09	47	5.9 – 7.8	SR	
β Per	03	08	+40	58	2.1 – 3.4	Ecl.	'Algol'

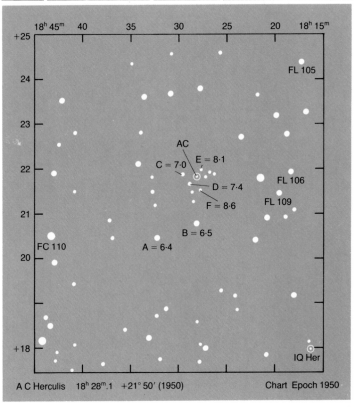

A C Herculis   18ʰ 28ᵐ.1   +21° 50′ (1950)   Chart Epoch 1950

'C(1)V(2)D', representing 'C, one-third, variable, two-thirds, D'. Other fractions could be given by '...(1)V(3)...', '...(3)V(2)...', '...(4)V(1)...', or whatever the case may warrant. Don't try to divide the interval into more than five parts, as errors then begin to creep in. Other methods can be used when you have gained experience.

You can obtain the actual, or deduced, magnitude by simple arithmetic. Take the difference between the two comparison stars, and work out one (or both) fractions. Remember that magnitude values increase for fainter stars, so add the fraction to the magnitude of the bright comparison, or subtract from that of the fainter, whichever is the easiest. Give the result to 0·1 magnitude.

This all sounds more complicated than it is in practice. Try it, and you will be pleasantly surprised. There are some problems, of course. Don't stare at red stars, otherwise they will seem to get brighter. Take short glimpses instead. (They always show far more difference between observers than bluer objects.) Try turning your head, because of two equal stars, the one that is 'noseward and downward' will always appear slightly brighter.

Novae

There are many forms of eruptive variables (mostly close binary systems) and outbursts of a large number of individual objects may be seen quite frequently, even though at irregular intervals. Novae, however, are an extreme form, sometimes rising by 10 magnitudes (10000 times brighter) or even more, in just a couple of days. However, it is not until a particular star erupts that it is even known to exist, so the outbursts are quite unpredictable. Once the star has been discovered it may be followed by the ordinary methods of estimating magnitudes, although there is usually the problem of finding suitable comparison stars and obtaining their magnitudes.

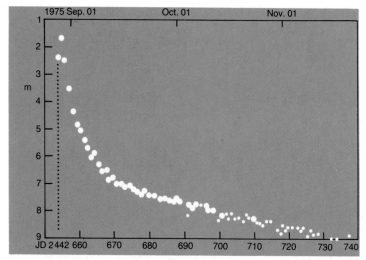

The light-curve of the bright, fast nova V 1500 Cyg that erupted in 1975.

Nova V 1500 Cyg at magnitude 2 (left) and at about magnitude 11 (right), many weeks into its decline.

It is obviously most important to discover these objects as soon as possible, so many amateurs undertake nova patrols, either visually or photographically. Like comet searching (page 169) it requires considerable patience to learn the stellar patterns over even a small area of the sky. All the other variable stars must also be recognized to prevent numerous 'false alarms'.

Photographs have the advantage of providing a permanent record, but must be taken in pairs to enable the inevitable emulsion faults to be detected. They also have to be developed and examined immediately if a nova is to be detected at an early stage.

Novae most frequently occur in the regions closest to the visible Milky Way, and various co-ordinated patrols keep close watch over these areas. Both these patrols and individual observers have recorded some notable successes over the years. The information which they have obtained has frequently been of vital interest to professional astronomers.

Double and multiple stars

Many stars appear close to one another in the sky. Some of these have no actual connection, being at greatly different distances and merely lying on the same line of sight. These are **optical doubles.** In other cases the stars are in orbit around one another, and form true **binary systems.** Multiple systems consisting of three or more stars also occur. Many doubles (of both types) are striking objects in binoculars or small telescopes. One or two, such as ζ Ursa Majoris (Mizar) with its companion Alcor, are reasonably easy for the naked eye. Eyesight alone will just about resolve ε Lyrae, but this is easily split with binoculars. In a small telescope with magnifications of 100-200, it is visible as four components.

The bright pair of stars α (left) and β Centauri. α Cen is multiple, with a close pair (mags 0 and 1·4), and 11th mag. Proxima Centauri far out in its orbit.

Double stars are an excellent test of telescopic resolution, and some suitable objects are given in the table. However, do not be unduly disappointed if you seem to fail completely to reach the theoretical resolution of your telescope – once again, considerable practice and excellent seeing conditions are required.

In true binaries the positions of the stars change as they orbit one another, but the brighter star is treated as fixed, and the relative position of the fainter is determined. If measurements are made over a period of years the orbit can be drawn. The shape and size of this depend upon the orientation in space. At times some pairs may be easily split, but at other times they close and become difficult objects.

Measuring double stars

The measurement of doubles really requires a long-focus telescope (refractors and catadioptrics are generally preferred), a proper mounting and drive, and a micrometer. There are several different forms of the latter, but the most readily understandable is the filar micrometer which incorporates fixed and moving wires (still frequently made from spider's web). The required measurements are **position angle** (PA) and separation, and because of the difficulty of obtaining the precise values (and instrumental errors), averages have to be taken of many individual measurements. Probably because of the problems and the instrumental requirements, this is a very neglected field of observation.

In many doubles the components are too close for them to be resolved directly through any telescope. However, when their spectra are examined, doubling of the lines shows that more than one star is involved. These **spectroscopic binaries** are very numerous. So many binary systems of both types exist that most stars are part of a multiple system. The Sun is most unusual in not having any stellar companion (as far as we know).

Double stars

Desig.	RA (2000)		Dec.		Mags.
	h	m	°	'	
γ And	02	04	+42	21	Multiple: 3.0, 5.0, 5.0, 6.2
ζ Aqr	22	29	−00	02	4.4, 4.6: white stars
γ Ari	01	54	+19	18	4.2, 4.4: white stars
ε Boo	14	45	+27	04	'Izar': 3.0, 6.3: orange & blue-green
ζ Cnc	08	12	+17	39	5.0, 5.5: fainter third component
α CVn	12	56	+38	19	3.2, 5.7
η Cas	00	49	+57	49	4.0, 7.6: yellow & red stars
α Cen	14	40	−60	51	0.0, 1.7: yellow stars
66 Cet	02	13	−02	24	6.0, 7.8
α Cru	12	27	−63	06	1.6, 2.1: blue-white stars
β Cyg	19	31	+37	57	3.0, 5.3: yellow & blue
γ Del	20	47	+16	08	4.0, 5.0: yellow stars
θ Eri	02	58	−40	18	3.4, 4.4: blue-white stars
α Her	17	15	+14	24	'Ras Algethi': 3.0, 6.1
γ Leo	10	19	+19	51	2.0, 3.5: yellow stars
ε Lyr	18	44	+39	40	'Double double': 4.6, 6.3; 4.9, 5.2
β Mon	06	29	−07	02	5.0, 5.5: white stars
η Per	02	51	+55	53	4.0, 8.5: orange & blue
β Sco	16	05	−19	48	2.0, 6.0: blue-white
δ Ser	15	35	+10	32	3.0, 4.0: white stars
ζ UMa	13	24	+54	55	'Mizar': 2.1, 4.2
γ Vel	08	09	−47	21	2.2, 4.8: blue-white; quadruple system
γ Vir	12	42	−01	27	3.0, 3.0: yellow-white stars
γ Vol	07	09	−70	30	3.9, 5.8: yellowish stars

Star clusters

Apart from the stars that occur in binary and multiple systems, many are found in distinct groups, known as clusters. There are two main types, the **open clusters** (often called galactic clusters) and the spherical **globular clusters**. The open clusters, in particular, are best seen in instruments that give a wide field of view.

OPEN CLUSTERS The open clusters are irregular in shape and are groups of stars that formed together from a single interstellar dust and gas cloud, and which thus have similar ages and compositions. They are mainly found in the spiral arms of our Galaxy (page 185) and as a result are concentrated in the regions of the Milky Way. These clusters vary greatly in the number of stars within them. Some may be difficult to distinguish from the surrounding star fields and just appear as slightly thicker patches of stars. These are often old clusters which have gradually spread out due to each star's individual motion and thus become less distinct. On the other hand, younger clusters, such as the Pleiades (M45) are often densely crowded and contain many hot, young stars.

GLOBULAR CLUSTERS Globular clusters are dense spheres of stars which sometimes contain millions of individual stars. They are very old and were formed very early in the history of the Galaxy itself, long before any heavy elements had been produced by nuclear fusion within stars and redistributed into space by their explosion. Unlike the open clusters they are not found in the spiral arms, but are concentrated around the centre of the Galaxy in the constellation of Sagittarius. They are also found far out in the galactic halo (page 185).

Clusters

Below: *The young, hot stars of the Pleiades open cluster, with blue reflection nebulosity*

Const.	Desig.
Aur	M38
Aur	M37
Cnc	M44
CVn	M3
Cas	M103
Cen	NGC 3766
Cen	ω
Cru	NGC 4755
Cyg	M39
Gem	M35
Her	M13
Lac	NGC 7243
Peg	M15
Per	h & χ
Per	M34
Sgr	M23
Sco	M6
Sco	M7
Scu	M11
Tau	M45
TrA	NGC 6025
Tuc	NGC 104

Above: *The globular cluster M13 in Hercules is one of the finest in the northern hemisphere of the sky.*

RA		Dec.		Type	Name or remarks
		(2000)			
h	*m*	°			
05	29	+35	51	Open	
05	52	+32	34	Open	
08	40	+19	41	Open	'Praesepe' – n.e.
13	42	+28	23	Globular	
01	33	+60	42	Open	field with red star
11	36	−61	37	Open	binocular object
13	27	−47	19	Globular	magnificent n.e. object
12	54	−60	21	Open	'Jewel Box' near red κ
21	32	+48	26	Open	bright object
06	09	+24	20	Open	binocular object
16	42	+36	27	Globular	finest northern globular
22	15	+49	45	Open	
21	30	+12	10	Globular	bright object
02	22	+57	08	Open	'Double Cluster' – n.e.
02	42	+42	47	Open	n.e. object
17	57	−19	01	Open	
17	40	−32	13	Open	n.e. object
17	54	−34	49	Open	bright – n.e.
18	51	−06	17	Open	'Wild Duck' – bright
03	47	+24	07	Open	'Pleiades' – n.e.
16	03	−60	29	Open	bright
00	24	−72	05	Globular	47 Tuc – n.e.

Nebulae

A large amount of gas and dust exists within the Galaxy and this is often concentrated into the dense clouds known as nebulae. These may be divided into several categories.

DARK NEBULAE In the dark nebulae thick masses of dust block the light from distant stars. There are several regions like this along the Milky Way, such as the Great Rift in Cygnus, and the Coalsack in Crux. Apart from these dense clouds, however, there are many fainter ones, very difficult to see, which wind their way across the general star clouds of the Galaxy. Low magnifications and excellent conditions are needed to reveal some of these faint dark lanes.

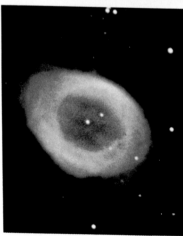

Nebulae

Const.	Desig.
Car	NGC 3372
Dor	NGC 2070
Dra	NGC 6543
Lyr	M57
Ori	M42
Per	M76
Sgr	M8
Sgr	M20
Sgr	M17
Tau	M1
UMa	M97
Vul	M27

REFLECTION NEBULAE Dust is also responsible for the reflection nebulae. There are not very many that can be seen by visual observers, but some of the nebulosity in the Pleiades may be glimpsed under good conditions. They are, however, often easy to see on long-exposure photographs. They usually appear blue; the clouds of dust reflect light from hot, young stars lying in front of them. Even though gas may be present, only in a few cases do the stars provide enough energy for it to glow.

Opposite: *The dark cloud of the Horsehead Nebula in Orion blocks the light from more distant stars.*

Opposite below: *The Ring Nebula in Lyra is a spectacular planetary nebula.*

Left: *The Great Nebula in Orion is the finest example of an emission nebula.*

RA		Dec.		Type	Name or remarks
		(2000)			
h	*m*	°			
10	45	−59	45	Emission	η Carinae nebula
06	39	−69	15	Emission	'Tarantula' – in LMC
17	59	+66	38	Planetary	−
18	54	+33	02	Planetary	'Ring'
05	35	−05	23	Emission	'Great Nebula'
01	42	+51	34	Planetary	(faint, mag. 12.2)
18	05	−24	20	Emission	'Lagoon'
18	02	−23	02	Emission	'Trifid'
18	21	−16	11	Emission	'Omega'
05	35	+22	01	SNR	'Crab'
11	15	+55	02	Planetary	'Owl'
20	00	+22	43	Planetary	'Dumbbell'

EMISSION NEBULAE   In the emission nebulae, ultraviolet light from stars within them is absorbed and re-emitted at visible wavelengths. To the eye they appear greenish, but photography shows the red of glowing hydrogen. The most notable example is the famous Orion Nebula (M42), just visible to the naked eye as a hazy 'star' in Orion's 'sword'. Telescopes reveal a vast glowing cloud of gas, surrounding the hot, young stars of the 'Trapezium' (θ Orionis). The emission and dark nebulae are often the regions where new stars are being formed.

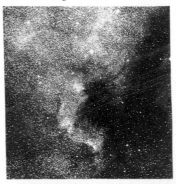

Left: *The North America Nebula in Cygnus is glowing hydrogen gas and the 'Gulf of Mexico' is a dark interstellar cloud.*

Below: *NGC 7293, the Helix Nebula in Aquarius, is a large and striking planetary nebula.*

PLANETARY NEBULAE   Another form of nebula is that formed when an evolving star gently sheds a shell of gas. These planetary nebulae (so named from their appearance) are also growing, and sometimes the small, hot star can be seen in the very centre. Similar nebulae may arise when very massive stars explode as supernovae (page 187), disrupting the stars and ejecting into space heavy elements formed within them. These elements may later be incorporated into new stars and planets. Such nebulae are known as **supernova remnants**, and the Crab Nebula in Taurus (M1) and the Veil Nebula, part of the enormous Cygnus Loop, are the most easily seen in amateur telescopes.

The Galaxy

M31 in Andromeda, a large Sb galaxy, is accompanied by several smaller, satellite systems.

The star clouds of the Milky Way run right around the sky. They are least distinct in the region of Gemini, Orion and Auriga, where they may be seen on only the darkest nights. In the other half of the sky, however, between Cygnus in the north and Carina in the south, a clear night will reveal densely-packed clouds of stars. In some areas the constellation patterns formed by the brightest stars may even be difficult to pick out from the brilliant background. Dark 'rifts' show the presence of dense clouds of dust, absorbing the light from the stars beyond them. All these clouds of stars and dust, as well as the young open clusters mark the plane of the spiral arms and the disk of our Galaxy. The diameter of this vast, thin disk is about 30 kiloparsecs or roughly 100 000 light-years.

Wide-angle photographs sometimes give an indication of our Galaxy's appearance as a disk with a central bulge, which lies in the general direction of the constellation of Sagittarius. This lens-shaped bulge is the **galactic nucleus**, a flattened ball of old, reddish stars, very distinct from the young, blue stars of the spiral arms. It surrounds the galactic centre, which lies far away in Sagittarius, close to the border with Ophiuchus. In visible light it is hidden from us by the dense clouds of dust in the galactic plane, but X-ray, infrared and radio observations reveal it to be the site of gigantic, swirling clouds of gas, huge star clusters, and in the very centre, what is probably an enormous black hole. Our Sun and Solar System lie well out towards the edge of the Galaxy, about 10 kiloparsecs (32 000 light-years) from the centre.

But there is yet another, even larger, but far less distinct, part of our Galaxy. This is the **galactic halo**, a vast sphere of space, stretching out beyond even the galactic disk, its indefinite boundaries marked by far-distant globular clusters. It also contains an unknown amount of gas, and a thinly-scattered collection of faint, individual stars.

How would the Galaxy appear from outside? Probably like the nearest large galaxy M31 (the Andromeda Galaxy), the more distant M81 in Ursa Major, or perhaps even somewhat like the famous, nearly edge-on galaxy M104 (the 'Sombrero') in Virgo, with its thin, dark band of obscuring dust.

Other galaxies

The galaxies are very varied in size and shape. Some are small and irregular, like the Small Magellanic Cloud, which merely appears as a detached part of the Milky Way. Others, such as the Large Magellanic Cloud, the nearest system to our own, are rather larger and show some slight organized structure.

Other galaxies may be broadly divided into two types: the spirals and the ellipticals, more properly called ellipsoidal galaxies.

Spiral galaxies are like our own, flattened systems with a disk, central nucleus, and hot, young stars. A few rare ones (the So galaxies) have no spiral arms, but in all the others the structure can usually be seen if the face of the disk is turned towards us. The loosely-wound arms of Sc galaxies like M33 in Triangulum are not so easy to make out in a telescope as the closer arms of Sb spirals such as the magnificent M81 in Ursa Major. The tighter Sa galaxies may appear almost structureless in amateur-sized telescopes, but show details in long-exposure photographs. In the **barred spiral galaxies** (SB) the arms grow out of the ends of a distinct bar across the centre: M95 in Leo, an SBb galaxy, is one example.

The smooth, **elliptical galaxies** contain only old stars, and very little gas and dust. They are classified by the letter E followed by a number to indicate the amount of flattening. The EO galaxies, like M87 the giant elliptical in Virgo, appear completely spherical. M49, also in Virgo, is more flattened and is an E4 galaxy. The most extreme cases, the E7 galaxies, are very rare. They may appear almost rectangular and like an edge-on spiral galaxy. The smallest, dwarf ellipsoidal galaxies may only have one-millionth of the mass of our Galaxy, while the large, giant ellipsoidals (like M87) may be more than 100 times as massive.

As the plane of our Galaxy is so heavily obscured by dust, we see most galaxies when looking out towards the Galactic Poles. This is especially the case in the northern hemisphere, where galaxies cluster thickly in the constellation of Coma Berenices and in nearby Virgo. Some of the most

Our view of NGC 253, an Sc galaxy in Sculptor, is nearly edge-on.

Galaxies

Const.	Desig.
And	M31
And	M32
CVn	M51
Dor/Men	LMC
Tri	M33
Tuc	SMC
UMa	M81
UMa	M101
Vir	M87

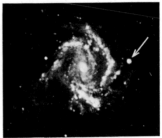

Left: M33 in Triangulum (type Sc) is viewed nearly face-on, but its outer arms are often difficult to detect.

Below: A fairly bright supernova (arrow) in a spiral arm of its parent galaxy.

notable visual (and photographic) objects are given in the table.

Galaxies provide a considerable challenge to astrophotographers, as they are usually dim and require long exposures and careful guiding for satisfactory pictures to be obtained. They may also be regularly watched, either visually or photographically, in a way similar to the nova patrols (page 177), for the outburst of **supernovae**.

SUPERNOVAE   These stellar explosions have not been recorded in our own galaxy since two events in 1572 and 1604 which were observed, respectively, by the famous astronomers Tycho Brahe and Johannes Kepler. But these outbursts are occasionally seen in other galaxies, and several have been discovered by amateurs. They are far greater than nova outbursts (page 176) and the stars may rise by 20 magnitudes or more. These stellar explosions may be so spectacular that for a brief period a single supernova may even far exceed the brightness of the whole of its galaxy, which may be a system of 100 thousand million stars.

RA		Dec.		Type	Name or remarks
		(2000)			
h	m	°	′		
00	43	+41	17	Sb	Great Andromeda Galaxy
00	43	+40	53	E2	companion to M31
13	30	+47	12	Sb	'Whirlpool'
05	20	−69	00	Irr	Large Magellanic Cloud
01	34	+30	39	Sc	large, nearby spiral
00	52	−73	14	Irr	Small Magellanic Cloud
09	56	+69	04	Sb	—
14	03	+54	21	Sc	—
12	31	+12	23	E0	giant elliptical

Bibliography

American Association of Variable Star Observers. *AAVSO Variable Star Atlas*. Cambridge, Massachusetts: Sky Publishing, 1980.

British Astronomical Asssociation:
Guide for Observers of the Moon. London, 1974.
Handbook. London, published annually.
Satellite Observers' Manual. London, 1974.
Star Charts. London, 1981.

Burnham, R. *Burnham's Celestial Handbook*. 3 vols. New York: Dover, 1978.

Duffet-Smith, P. *Practical Astronomy with Your Calculator*. 2nd edition. Cambridge, England: Cambridge University Press, 1981.

Eastman Kodak Co. *Astrophotography Basics*. Publication AC–48. Rochester, New York, 1980.

King-Hele, D. *Observing Earth Satellites*. London: Macmillan, 1983.

Moore, P., editor. *Practical Amateur Astronomy*. Guildford, England: Lutterworth Press, 1975.

Norton, A. P. *Norton's Star Atlas*. 17th edition. Edited by G. S. Satterthwaite. Edinburgh: Gall & Inglis, 1978.

Royal Astronomical Society of Canada. *Observer's Handbook*. Toronto, published annually.

Sidgwick, J. B. *Observational Astronomy for Amateurs*. 4th edition. Edited by J. Muirden. London: Pelham, 1982.

Tirion, W. *Sky Atlas 2000*. Cambridge, Massachusetts: Sky Publishing, 1981.

Journals and Magazines

Astronomy. AstroMedia Corp., PO Box 92788, Milwaukee, Wisconsin (monthly).

Journal. British Astronomical Association, Burlington House, Piccadilly, London W1V 0NL (bimonthly).

Popular Astronomy. Junior Astronomical Society, 36 Sandown Way, Greenham, Newbury, Berks. RG14 7SD (quarterly).

Quarterly Journal. Royal Astronomical Society, Burlington House, Piccadilly, London W1V 0NL (quarterly).

Sky & Telescope. Sky Publishing, 49 Bay State Road, Cambridge, Massachusetts 02138 (monthly).

The Astronomer, 177 Thunder Lane, Thorpe St. Andrew, Norwich NR7 0JF (amateur observations, monthly).

Organizations

United Kingdom:

British Astronomical Association. Burlington House, Piccadilly, London W1V 0NL.

British Interplanetary Society. 27–29 South Lambeth Road, London SW8 1SZ.

Junior Astronomical Society. 36 Sandown Way, Greenham, Newbury, Berks. RG14 7SD.

Royal Astronomical Society. Burlington House, Piccadilly, London W1V 0NL.

North America

American Association of Variable Star Observers. 187 Concord Avenue, Cambridge, Massachusetts 02138.

American Meteor Society. Dept. of Physics and Astronomy, SUNY, Genesco, New York 14454.

Association of Lunar and Planetary Observers. Box 3AZ, University Park, New Mexico 88003.

Astronomical League. PO Box 12821, Tucson, Arizona 85732 (for addresses of local societies).

Astronomical Society of the Pacific. 1290 24th Avenue, San Francisco, California 94122.
Royal Astronomical Society of Canada. 136 Dupont Street, Toronto, Ontario M5R 1V2.
Western Amateur Astronomers. PO Box 2316, Palm Desert, California 92261 (for addresses of local societies).
Other countries
Astronomical Society of New South Wales. PO Box 208, Eastwood, N.S.W. 2122, Australia.
Astronomical Society of South Australia. PO Box 199, Adelaide, S. Australia 501.
Astronomical Society of Southern Africa. c/o South African Astronomical Observatory, PO Box 9, Observatory, 7935, Cape Republic of South Africa.
Astronomical Society of Victoria. PO Box 1059J, Melbourne, Victoria 3001.
British Astronomical Association (New South Wales Branch). Sydney Observatory, Sydney, N.S.W. 2001.
Royal Astronomical Society of New Zealand. PO Box 3181, Wellington C1.

INDEX

Page numbers in *italics* refer to illustrations.